childbirth instructor™

MAGAZINE'S

guide to

CAREERS IN BIRTH

How to Have a Fulfilling Job in Pregnancy, Labor, and Parenting Support without a Medical Degree

SUZANNE B. ROBOTTI
MARGARET ANN INMAN

John Wiley & Sons, Inc.

New York • Chichester • Weinheim • Brisbane • Singapore • Toronto

This book is printed on acid-free paper.♾

Published by John Wiley & Sons, Inc.
Published simultaneously in Canada.

Library of Congress Cataloging-in-Publication Data

Robotti, Suzanne B.
Childbirth instructor magazine's guide to careers in birth : how to have a fulfilling job in pregnancy, labor, & parenting support without a medical degree / by Suzanne B. Robotti and Margaret Ann Inman.
p. cm.
Includes index.
ISBN 0-471-16230-2 (alk. paper)
1. Childbirth—Study and teaching—Vocational guidance.
2. Parenting—Study and teaching—Vocational guidance. I. Inman, Margaret Ann. II. Childbirth instructor magazine.
III. Title. IV. Title: Guide to careers in birth.
RG973.R6 1998
618.2'023—DC21 97-16996

Printed in the United States of America.

10 9 8 7 6 5 4 3 2 1

CONTENTS

INTRODUCTION

Do you love babies? Does the sight of a stroller have you koo-che-cooing (even if it embarrasses you)? Does your hand reach out to pat strange women's pregnant bellies? And don't you love to be around glowing pregnant mothers? Make your career the birth field, and you'll be surrounded by bouncing babies, happily nervous daddies-to-be, and women growing into motherhood.

How can you fit into this picture? Expectant and new parents are surrounded by a professional support structure that was not necessary as recently as two generations ago and was not even dreamed of one generation ago. And, unlike many of the innovations that modern times have brought, this new support structure is a good thing. It is a positive response to the mechanization of birth and the isolation of daily life.

Historically women were surrounded by family and friends. Experienced women offered comfort remedies and psychological support during pregnancy and labor. Birth took place at home, where the laboring woman felt safe and where she was cared for by loving people she had known her entire life. Extended families supplied grandparents to guide and develop early parenting skills (and to provide the buffer and break parents occasionally need from their own children).

Last year, nearly 4 million women gave birth. In some areas, such as childbirth, women routinely receive education and support. Other aspects of pregnancy and early parenting education, such as pregnancy exercise classes, are not yet commonplace and have lots of growth potential as an industry and a career.

Become a support person in the birthing process: You could train to become a childbirth educator, a lactation consultant (a person who helps women breastfeed), or both—more than 60 percent of all childbirth educators are also lactation consultants. You could take a field in which you are already proficient and apply it to mothers and babies—an aerobics instructor (or exercise enthusiast) can be certified to teach pregnancy fitness; a CPR instructor can train to teach infant CPR and the full range of infant first aid. But one step at a time. First focus on what makes you feel happy, because that is what this industry is all about!

As you flip through this book, note the box at the beginning of each chapter. In it are outlined the considerations and the requirements of each job so you can see if it fits your life needs: Does it meet your interests? Will it pay enough? Will you have the necessary flexibility in your schedule? Are you willing to commit to the appropriate training?

The purpose of this book is not to provide job training but to introduce you to your options in the various careers that support birth. Birth can be an empowering, growing experience. And you can be a crucial part of it. Best of all, you won't need eight years of medical school plus tens of thousands of dollars in tuition to participate.

This book was written with the loving and unending support of both of our husbands and in honor of those women who faced childbearing bravely for our sakes, our mothers.

We thank Nicholas Smith for seeing us through this with wisdom and understanding.

1

HELPING POTENTIAL PARENTS PLAN AHEAD: PRECONCEPTION COUNSELOR/EDUCATOR

What will you do?	Provide nutrition, financial, and lifestyle information that promotes healthy pregnancies
How many hours a week?	3–15 hours (1–5 classes per week)
Your work hours?	Variable; not traditional
Will you need licensing/ certification?	None required
What can you earn?	$20 per couple
Liability insurance needed?	None required

Planning on becoming pregnant? Preconception *counseling*? Those were not options for our grandmothers. But now, preconception counseling allows couples to think about what they're getting into and to plan for a comfortable, safe pregnancy and a healthy child. And, with reproductive technology more advanced than we could ever have imagined, preconception counseling can help couples with fertility problems become informed about new ways to start a family.

So if you are interested in providing adult education and in helping women plan for a healthy pregnancy and birth, the recent interest in preconception health may present an exciting new career opportunity. We're not talking about *genetic* counseling—a profession that may require an advanced degree in the sciences—but about helping parents to plan for the most important event in their lives, to consider issues of preconception and first-trimester health prior to conventional childbirth education classes.

WHY COUPLES WAIT

Past generations did not have the freedom to plan when they wanted to be parents. Before modern birth control was available, women often had children throughout their childbearing years. Then, during World War II, most women delayed their childbearing until peacetime. After the war, a record number of babies were born to older women. Not long after that came the baby boom, when the brides of returning soldiers started having children early and often.

Most American women are now having their first child not by accident or by necessity, but by choice. They are devoting more time to their education or professional life before, or in place of, following what used to be the expected sequence of events in a woman's life: developing a relationship, getting married, and having children. Then, when they are ready to have a family, they hope to beat the biological clock.

Other women are having babies later in life not because they are postponing pregnancy, but because they are having trouble becoming pregnant. Some aspiring parents find that conceiving is not as easy as they expected. Now, however, new fertility methods have made childbearing a possibility for many otherwise childless couples. Thanks to new and astounding technology, parents can often accomplish what seemed impossible by conventional means. Some parents succeed beyond expectations and give birth to twins or triplets.

With these new populations of first-time parents on the rise, those interested in catering to their needs have a unique opportunity to fill a gap in prechildbirth education.

WHAT COUPLES WANT

Reflecting on their lives, most parents point to the birth of their children as the cornerstone of their lives—what really counted when all was said and done. Yet for generations, most parents have approached this momentous event with naiveté, with only vague ideas about how to minimize the risks and maximize the outcome for the healthiest, happiest children they could bring into the world. Pregnancy and childbirth were an expected and usually joyous part of marriage. The only alternative for parents who couldn't conceive was adoption.

Now, many parents are thinking more about what they're getting into. They're not stumbling into pregnancy and parenthood. They're learning about it and planning it, not only for the health of their child, but also for the happiness and stability of their marriage. For couples who have fertility problems, highly effective fertility drugs and techniques such as in vitro fertilization have dramatically increased their chances of becoming parents. Preconception counselors can help advise parents about these issues.

Improved knowledge and changing attitudes have also revolutionized obstetrical care. In earlier generations, when a woman came to the doctor suspecting she was pregnant, she was only one patient. Today, health care providers realize that when they see an expectant mother, they're seeing two patients: one adult and one unborn. And even the term *patient* may be inappropriate, for modern physicians are beginning to view pregnancy not as an illness but as a natural condition that may require care—though not always medical treatments.

THE TWELVE-MONTH PREGNANCY

Most women take good care of their health once they know they're pregnant. But there is a lot they can do for themselves and their child in the months before they become pregnant. This prepregnancy period was not a concern in generations past; the cause-and-effect relationship of what's done in the months before pregnancy went unexamined primarily because no one realized its importance. Now we do. Women can plan to eliminate unhealthful habits, such as smoking, well before they become pregnant. They can get immunizations so that many diseases will not pose a risk to mother or fetus during pregnancy. They can start taking folic acid in the months before pregnancy to protect against neural tube defects such as spina bifida. They can undergo screening procedures that can give crucial information to help them plan for the health and quality of life for their children.

We are living in a revolutionary time in communications technology as well. Women are better educated than at any time in history. Mass communication allows more people to know about things simultaneously. Society as a whole is more health conscious. Women are more able and willing to do what needs to be done to bring healthy babies into their lives.

Ideas of responsibility have also changed. Women desensitized to the medical profession's record of treating pregnancy as an illness now know that they don't have to accept this view. Women are claiming their right to choose birth methods, to determine who will be present during birth, to decide on the size of their families, and to recenter pregnancy and childbearing on their terms.

Doctors are also reevaluating well-entrenched views and procedures. They now realize that their goal should be keeping patients well—not just treating them when they're sick. They know they don't run the entire show during pregnancy. Women and their partners may ask about their options in childbirth, rather than just accepting what the doctor says will be done.

In summary, expectations have never been higher about the prospects for having a baby and about the means of safely becoming pregnant. Changes in society and in technology have revolutionized women's approach to pregnancy. Now they can plan ahead.

WHY PRECONCEPTION CLASSES?

You may be convinced of the critical role of preconception education, but it's not yet a routine part of childbirth education in most communities. How do you convince potential clients about the importance of including preconception education as a routine part of their childbirth education? Here are some arguments:

- Being well informed about the pregnancy increases the chances of having a healthy baby. This is a particularly important concern for the woman in her thirties or forties who as yet has no children and who may be concerned about the increased risks unique to what the medical profession inelegantly calls the "elderly primipara." It is also a particular concern for women who have a family history of genetic illness that might affect the health of the next generation.
- The fetus is most vulnerable to environmental hazards in the first trimester. During this period, cell organization, cell differentiation, and organ development take place. These processes can be threatened by, for example, an infection, certain drugs, nutritional deficiencies, or illness and by exposure to such hazards as smoke, pesticides, or paint fumes. And in our technological world, the environmental hazards keep multiplying. Mothers can do their best to ensure the normal development of the baby by being aware of the hazards and trying to avoid them.

- Conception may not be as easy for some women as for others. Older women might not get pregnant for a year, whereas younger women might conceive immediately. Preconception counseling and classes can teach the striving preparents how to maximize their chances of conceiving.

- Preconception counseling can inform partners who are considering procedures such as in vitro fertilization about what is involved and what the costs and the chances of success will be.

- Those who are contemplating parenthood because of pressures from family or friends may have the opportunity to rethink their reasons for wanting to become parents.

- Couples who are unsure about the financial ramifications of fertility procedures, pregnancy, and raising a child can examine just what their obligations will be.

WHO ARE MY LIKELY CLIENTS?

Those interested in preconception planning are often older and may have a more mature sense of themselves and of the importance of good health. These women and their partners are often very goal-directed. They approach pregnancy as they might a business plan: project pregnancy. They are thirsty for knowledge on childbirth and parenting. This means that the preconception educator must be well prepared to answer a variety of relatively sophisticated and often specific questions about pregnancy and childbirth.

Likely Candidates for Preconception Classes

- Older couples contemplating a first child
- Younger couples wanting more information before becoming pregnant

continued

- Couples with infertility problems
- Those with (or with a family history of) conditions such as:

  Anemia

  Asthma

  Cystic fibrosis

  Diabetes

  Epilepsy or seizures

  Heart conditions, such as rheumatic heart disease, mitral valve prolapse, or congenital heart defects

  Hemophilia

  High blood pressure

  Kidney disease, especially if requiring dialysis

  Phenylketonuria (PKU) (may cause miscarriages or birth defects)

  Sexually transmitted diseases

  Sickle-cell disease (most common in black women)

  Stomach disorders, such as ulcers

  Systemic lupus erythematosus (may cause repeated miscarriages)

  Thyroid disorders (may affect fertility)

Other potential clients may be motivated because they have a chronic condition or know of a family history of medical problems that might affect their pregnancy. They want more information about their chances for a healthy pregnancy and a healthy child.

Still others may simply want to know more about what's in store for them: everything from their most fertile times to financial considerations. These are issues that a well-prepared, well-informed preconception counselor should be able to handle.

WHAT WILL I BE TEACHING?

Preconception classes generally provide information on the important health and lifestyle habits that should be considered and, if necessary, changed in the months before the contemplated conception. Among the topics that should be covered are:

- Nutrition   Eating right is one of the best and most important things an expectant mom or a hopeful mom can do for her baby.

- Health hazards   Smoking, alcohol, certain medications, certain diseases, and job-related hazards may harm a developing fetus.

- Family medical history   A complete and detailed family health history of both parents will help the couple to anticipate potential complications resulting from genetic diseases or chronic conditions.

- Work environment   Assessing and minimizing the possibility of exposure to environmental toxins helps ensure development of fetus. Evaluating working conditions (for example, traveling, standing for long periods, driving, irregular hours) allows for planning ahead for comfort in the workplace during pregnancy.

- Genetic counseling   Parents-to-be need to know what it can tell them about their chances of a healthy pregnancy and baby.

- Prenatal testing   Potential parents will want to know what is involved, why a test is performed, and what test results can tell you about your child. Class profile will determine which tests should be emphasized; for example, amniocentesis and chorionic villus sampling in a class with predominantly older women.

- Lifestyle considerations   Parents contemplating pregnancy are urged to think about the impact the pregnancy and baby will have on their often well-established work, marriage, and lifestyle patterns. They should start thinking about child care options if the mother will be returning to work.

- Financial expectations during pregnancy, childbirth, and after. (See complete sample curriculum on page 17.)

WHAT'S THE FIRST STEP?

The first step is your own education in preconception matters. Some background in adult education is a big plus, probably a necessity, if you're to teach preconception classes. You may want to consult your local college to find out if there are courses that provide the medical/scientific information you'll need, particularly courses in women's health.

While no certification is required for teaching preconception classes, hospitals or clinics where you might teach may have requirements. Contact them. They may already be offering preconception classes as a part of their comprehensive childbirth education program. Find out what kind of training and certification are required of the educators there. If classes aren't available yet, find out from the hospital's gynecology department what sort of preconception counseling is available and whether the physicians there would consider referring the women they see who are contemplating pregnancy to your proposed preconception education program. Local midwives or nurse practitioners who have well-woman care may be a good resource for both information and prospective clients.

Develop a class curriculum. The curriculum on pages 14–17 is but a template to allow you to think about what should be included.

Your preconception classes, in order to be attractive to many of today's striving parents-to-be, must be kept short. This means packing enormous amounts of information into just one or two sessions of two or three hours each. Motivated couples will probably be willing to come for two sessions: one devoted to lifestyle changes and one to medical considerations. Couples considering in vitro fertilization or other high-tech methods of conception might want a special class. If there is a fertility clinic in your community, there may be an audience for such a specialized class.

WHERE DO I WORK?

Most likely, you'll be working within a comprehensive childbirth education program. If so, the likely locale is a hospital, women's center, physician's or midwife's office, or community center. A classroom-style setting is common. Feel free to rearrange; chairs placed in a circle are usually the most comfortable arrangement.

HOW MUCH DO I CHARGE?

The common charge for this class is $20 to $35 per session, with perhaps five or six couples per session.

WHAT SUPPLIES WILL I NEED?

Many of the materials used for childbirth classes are appropriate for preconception classes. These include charts showing the different stages of pregnancy, childbirth videotapes, and demonstration materials. (If you will be teaching in a hospital, it might already have the materials.) In addition, however, you will need supplies not used in childbirth classes: home pregnancy tests (for demonstration and discussion), fertility calculators, fact sheets on procedures such as amniocentesis and chorionic villus sampling, and healthful-eating menus for prepregnancy and early pregnancy.

The March of Dimes actively promotes preconception health care and is an excellent resource for adult education brochures and videotapes.

HOW DO I FIND CLIENTS?

To get the class started, you should be able to present a class outline to prospective parents and a full curriculum to hospital administrators who may want to determine the suitability of this addition to their educational program (see pages 14–17). Be prepared to provide specific details of what you plan to include in the course. Many hospitals have a formal proposal-and-review process for any addition to their educational offerings.

Urge local gynecologists or the gynecology department at the local hospital to refer their patients to preconception classes as soon as the possibility of pregnancy is mentioned. Stress that this class is not a substitute for preconception medical care or genetic counseling but an informational program to encourage parents-to-be to start out parenting on the right foot. Gynecologists and ob-gyns are some of the busiest medical professionals around; they may be delighted to learn that they can focus on the medical aspects of a potential pregnancy, while referring potential parents to another resource that will address their other concerns about conception, pregnancy, childbirth, and parenting.

Nurse-midwives offering well-woman care are also an excellent referral resource. Provide these health care professionals with information about your classes.

Prepare some brochures to market your classes. Try to use a hook such as a clever title, something like "Project: Pregnancy" or "Baby? Maybe!" Focus your information on the importance of preparing for pregnancy; promote preconception education as an essential component of prenatal education for modern couples. Describe the networking possibilities with others facing the same concerns they have.

Interest in preconception education is widespread. Contact your local newspaper and suggest it as a topic for a feature article with you, of course, offering your own insight and giving the local angle on educational opportunities. Volunteer to be a resource. At the very least, see if you can have your classes listed in any "Meetings" section.

You have a great opportunity to assist potential parents in preparing for the biggest event in their lives. Never have couples been so willing to participate in ensuring a healthy pregnancy, delivery, and child.

Most healthy adults do not need sophisticated genetic counseling; what they may want is information, reassurance, and resources. You can provide that, and without an advanced medical degree.

The key to establishing yourself as a preconception counselor is finding clients early enough. Childbirth education comes near the end of pregnancy—but preconception education can help lead to that happy time when parents are actually anticipating childbirth.

SAMPLE CLASS CURRICULUM

I. Introduction: Importance of preconception planning

A. Psychosocial aspects

Why do you want to have a baby?

Are you prepared?

B. Medical aspects

What are the chances of becoming pregnant?

How soon?

What family history characteristic can affect my pregnancy?

II. Discussion of goals

A. Familiarize parents with the concept of planning a pregnancy and the benefits of planning ahead

B. Dispel unfounded fears

C. Educate parents on the importance of a healthful lifestyle *before* conception to maximize the chances of a full-term pregnancy, a healthy birth, and a healthy child

D. Raise awareness of medical conditions and genetic factors that might affect the course (or the possibility) of pregnancy

E. Motivate couples to seek individual preconception counseling and advice from their health care provider or to seek genetic counseling

III. Work issues

A. Assess environmental hazards and safety concerns (for example, video display terminals)

B. Assess type of work performed and how it will be affected by pregnancy

C. Examine workplace for level of comfort

D. Investigate and understand medical coverage and disability

E. Evaluate financial considerations

F. Discuss return-to-work considerations

IV. Personal/lifestyle issues

A. Changes in relationships with pregnancy/family; need for communication

B. Mood swings during pregnancy and postpartum period

C. Adjustments to parenthood

V. Medical/health issues and changes

A. Healthful lifestyles

1. Nutrition
2. Vitamin supplements
3. Weight gain
4. Exercise
5. Avoiding substance abuse (including alcohol and smoking)

B. Age issues

1. The biological clock

   How real is it?

   How long might it take to become pregnant?

2. Genetic disorders (for example, Down's syndrome) and age-related risks

C. Obstetrical issues

1. Infertility
2. History of miscarriage
3. C-section
4. Uterine disorders (including fibroids)

D. Medical history

1. What your family history can reveal
2. How to gather your family medical history

   Offer resources and ideas for lost or shielded adoptee history

E. Medical conditions that can affect your pregnancy

F. Exercise

1. Current regimen
2. A program for pregnancy

G. Testing for medical disorders/genetic defects

1. Disorders found in ethnic groups (for example, sickle-cell anemia in African Americans)
2. Familial disorders
3. Special risks for older parents

H. What to expect from genetic counseling

I. Choosing an obstetrician

VI. Costs

A. Genetic counseling

B. Pregnancy care

C. Labor and delivery

D. Estimated costs of raising a child

VII. Childbirth education offerings

A. Options and programs (such as Bradley versus Lamaze)

B. Birthing options (birthing center, hospital, and so on)

C. Other classes (newborn care, breastfeeding, working and parenting, and so on)

VIII. Feedback and questions and answers

RESOURCES

BOOKS

Before You Conceive: The Complete Prepregnancy Guide by John R. Sussman and B. Blake Levitt. New York: Bantam Books, 1989.

The Pregnant Woman's Comfort Guide: Safe, Quick, and Easy Relief from the Discomforts of Pregnancy and Postpartum by Sherry L. M. Jimenez. New York: Avery Publishing Group, 1992.

Welcome to Club Mom by Leslie Lehr Spirson. Deerhaven, MN: Meadowbrook Press, 1994.

The Long-Awaited Stork: A Guide to Parenting after Infertility by Ellen Glazer. San Francisco: Lexington Books, 1994.

Staying Home Instead: Alternatives to the Two-Paycheck Family by Christine Davidson. New York: Macmillan, 1992.

Preconception: A Woman's Guide to Preparing for Pregnancy and Parenthood by Brenda Aikey-Keller. Santa Fe, NM: John Muir Publications, 1990.

SUPPLIES AND CATALOGS

Childbirth Graphics
P.O. Box 21207
Waco, TX 76702-1207
800-299-3366
World Wide Web site: http://www.wrsgroup.com
Call to order a free catalog of childbirth education materials, including books, flip charts, models, videotapes, and more.

ORGANIZATIONS

Formerly Employed Mothers at the Leading Edge
Nonprofit organization with network of seventy local support groups. $20 membership fee includes a subscription to the monthly newsletter. For more information, send a self-addressed stamped envelope to FEMALE, P.O. Box 31, Elmhurst, IL 60126.

March of Dimes
Birth Defects Foundation
P.O. Box 1657
Wilkes-Barre, PA 18703
800-367-6630
Fax: 717-825-1987
Public and professional educational materials about preconception counseling, genetic counseling, maternal/child health, and birth defects.

National Center for Education in Maternal and Child Health
2000 15th Street North
Suite 701
Arlington, VA 22201-2617
703-524-7802
Provides educational materials, and publishes guides, directories, and bibliographies in the area of maternal and child health. Processes information requests from the public, health care professionals, and businesses.

Foresight-American Foundation
5724 Clymer Road
Quakertown, PA 18951
214-529-9025
An organized program that identifies and reduces reproductive risks before conception and prepares both parents and the family for pregnancy and childbearing.

2

PREPARING WOMEN FOR LABOR AND PARENTING: CHILDBIRTH EDUCATOR

What will you do?	Teach childbirth preparation and parenting classes
How many hours a week?	3–12 hours in class, 1–2 hours preparation for class and paperwork, phone-call questions
Your work hours?	Not traditional; evenings and weekends
Will you need licensing/ certification?	None required, but available from several groups
What can you earn?	$50–$100 per couple per class series
Liability insurance needed?	No personal insurance required

TEACHING PREGNANT WOMEN

Childbirth education is one of the most successful consumer movements ever seen in America. Just a generation ago, fathers weren't allowed in the labor room, and women were routinely administered "twilight sleep," a spinal anesthesia of uncertain safety for both the mother and the baby. By the early 1960s, several different childbirth-related groups had formed independently in different parts of the United States: Lamaze in the New York City area, Read in Northern California, Bradley in Southern California. (Each group and method is discussed in the section Training and Certification.) They had the same underlying goal: to educate women about normal labor and delivery and to make them aware of the choices available to them. This movement was initially feared and fought by the established medical community. Traditional medical care is based on the doctor controlling the procedure. Labor and delivery is one of the few times when medical attention is called in for a natural, healthy function of the human body. It took some persuading to remind doctors that women are well, not sick, when having a baby.

As a childbirth educator you can truly change the world. Educators reach couples just as they are facing life changes. These couples are open to new ideas and desperately want information. Childbirth educators are teachers who can and do introduce innovations that change society. For example, twenty-five years ago car seats for children were uncommon, even difficult to find. Childbirth educators led the movement toward safety for infants by teaching parents-to-be about the benefits of car seats. Now car seats are required in all fifty states, and countless infant lives have been saved.

Lamaze became the best known of the childbirth preparation classes. Like all groups at the time, Lamaze classes focused on natural—unmedicated—delivery. However, some drugs have been developed that aren't as threatening to the health of either the mother or the baby as the ones used years ago, and many women now choose to use some drugs during labor. Childbirth classes have adjusted to the changing needs of women and routinely include a wide range of information. A childbirth educator will teach about preparation for parenting, coping skills for parenting, hospital procedures, discomforts of late pregnancy, sex during pregnancy and after birth, unexpected outcomes, breastfeeding, car seats, and diapering, not to mention labor and delivery. But the most important skill an educator teaches is life-coping skills. You will teach parents techniques to help them deal with pain, fear, and decisions. By doing that you will prepare them to become better parents.

The childbirth educator is the person to whom a pregnant woman turns for answers to medical and personal questions. She is a key medical authority for expectant and new mothers, especially because obstetricians send their clients to childbirth classes. That referral from obstetricians makes childbirth educators part of the woman's medical team and confers the authority of the doctor onto the educator. By sending pregnant women to classes, obstetricians have found that they spend less time answering questions on labor, delivery, and parenting. The average obstetrical appointment for a pregnant woman is only 15.5 minutes. Such short appointment times discourage questions and conversation with the doctor. Childbirth class becomes her opportunity to ask questions about all her seemingly minor concerns.

Many first-time mothers also aren't comfortable asking the pediatrician what the mother considers unimportant questions during the first weeks after the baby is born. Until the baby has gone through several visits with the pediatrician (which might take several months with a healthy baby), the new mother doesn't know the pediatrician well. She will often call her childbirth educator rather than bother the doctor. The childbirth educator is often accessible, friendly, and knowledgeable.

CHILDBIRTH EDUCATION

Nearly all first-time pregnant women attend childbirth classes at their obstetrician's urging. Women are scheduled to attend childbirth class in the last trimester of pregnancy. Each woman is encouraged to bring a support person, usually her spouse or a companion, who will be with her during labor and delivery. This support person is critical as the coach who helps the pregnant mother practice the pain-coping techniques taught in class and stays with her during her entire labor and birth. Childbirth class is not only to prepare the mother, but also to prepare the coach.

In addition to providing information, childbirth classes have another important function: they bring groups of pregnant women and their partners together to share their thoughts and experiences. The group experience helps couples make the emotional transition to being parents and exposes them to other couples going through the same process. To encourage interaction between the couples, classes are kept small (on average, ten couples). Plenty of time will be structured into the classes for couples to meet and speak with each other, during group projects in class, during the juice-and-cookie break, and during the mingling time before and after class. Many educators hold a reunion class scheduled a month after all the babies are due. It helps class members reestablish ties, and the friendships built in class often last years.

Traditionally, classes meet one night a week for six consecutive weeks, and each class lasts about two hours. They are usually scheduled for evenings and weekends so that both the pregnant woman and her coach can attend without interfering with their day jobs. There is a consumer demand for compacted classes, for the entire series to be given in one weekend, for example, or by videotape in the couples' homes. This has caused controversy among educators who resist this trend because of the social/emotional aspects that need time to develop. Some are bowing to public pressure and offering classes in varying lengths and times. Whether taught leisurely or in a marathon, the class series contains about twelve hours of teaching time.

WHAT WILL I BE TEACHING?

The basic topics you will cover are conditions of pregnancy, signs of labor and labor management, delivery and anesthesia options, and hospital procedures. (See complete sample class outline on pages 38–43.) After the first class, each class usually begins with a review and a practice session of labor-coping techniques—the famous breathing exercises and other pain-coping/distraction skills such as visualization, effleurage (a touch or stroke with the fingertips that glides over the abdomen during labor), massage, and water therapy. The new topic for the evening is presented in a 15-minute lecture, with time for questions and discussions. Following that might be a 5- to 10-minute video and then the juice-and-cookie break. New exercises will be introduced, and another lecture on a new topic leads into breaking the class into smaller groups for projects or ice-breaking games. For two or three of the evenings, the educator will try to schedule a guest lecturer for one of the segments. A popular guest lecturer is a graduate couple who bring their baby to class and discuss the realities of labor and parenting. The two hours usually go too quickly because the routine will be constantly interrupted by questions, both on and off the topic.

Information is presented in lectures of no longer than fifteen minutes, and educators try to use different methods to get the information across. Lectures, question-and-answer sessions, videos, reading assignments, small-group projects, quizzes, and guest lecturers are ways of keeping the couples alert while absorbing massive amounts of information. Spreading the exercises out into at least two sessions during each class gives pregnant women a chance to stretch and move. Women in advanced pregnancy are constantly carrying a large weight, and their bodies are tired. If you don't get them to move around every thirty minutes or so, you'll find them falling asleep during your lecture! The ice-breakers and small-group projects give the couples time to interact with each other and build the basis of friendships and support groups. The break is another time for socializing, as well as for trips to the restroom.

Several months after the class series ends, many educators hold a reunion class. Couples are told this class is merely a social occasion, a chance to show off their baby and to tell their labor-and-delivery story. But it has an important role. Not only does it help reestablish a support group for the new parents, but it also gives educators a chance to start a discussion on parenting topics and well-baby care and to spot and redirect parents who might be having difficulty coping with the transition to parenting. All new parents need to develop their own support networks. You should have several resources on hand, such as lactation consultants and new mother groups.

As mentioned in the previous section, compacted classes—"Lamaze in a Weekend"—are in demand by upscale, dual-career couples. The classes take place in a hotel starting Saturday morning and ending early Sunday evening. (The course charge includes one night's stay in the hotel.) The problems inherent in such a nontraditional class series become apparent quickly. In a weekend class, educators need to cover six hours of information a day. The childbirth educator is challenged to keep the couples interested during the long class periods. Couples get tired of looking at a childbirth educator who merely lectures, and their retention will drop quickly. Women have difficulty sitting still for long periods of time because their increased weight slows their circulation, leading to leg cramps and drowsiness. They also need to urinate frequently. Friendly relationships don't have time to form, so the social/support aspect of the series is lost. Still, some educators point out that some childbirth education is better than none, and they are afraid that these busy couples will become drop-outs if the six-week series is their only option.

Burnout, from teaching the same topics over and over in six-week increments, is an industrywide problem. Educators mention that the freshness of each new group of couples keeps them involved. However, most childbirth educators also teach related classes for grandparent and sibling preparation, and they go on for further training in order to teach breastfeeding or exercise classes.

WHAT'S THE FIRST STEP?

If you decide you want to become a childbirth educator, you should have an outgoing personality, be naturally social and gregarious, and find that you get involved easily in group dynamics. Because the content of the classes is repetitive for the educator, you will find yourself bored unless you can become personally involved and concerned about your clients, pregnant women and their partners.

As a childbirth educator, you are foremost a teacher. Beyond learning all the factual information about late pregnancy, birth, and parenting, you will need to develop your presentation skills and to learn how to lead discussions and control group dynamics. Oddly, most educators have to learn the teaching skills on the job because the traditional training for childbirth educators focuses on the medical aspects, not the educational.

Because the course content covers such a variety of technical and emotional information, childbirth educators often have highly diverse backgrounds.

The typical childbirth educator is a woman in her thirties who has had one or more children herself. Most childbirth educators developed an interest in childbirth preparation because the birthing experience was important to them; it was either very good (and she wants to help other women have positive, empowering birth experiences) or very bad (and she wants to help women avoid the disappointment, pain, and unhappiness she experienced). Educators will often comment that they love babies and that teaching classes is their way of keeping in touch with the birth experience and gives them their "baby fix." Usually, teaching classes is her primary personal (not family) income.

WHAT DO I CHARGE?

Independent educators charge from $50 to $100 per couple per class series based on how affluent their area is and what other educators are charging. Some educators suggest charging about 10 percent of what an obstetrician charges. If you teach for a group or hospital, a rate will be set for you. You will probably receive substantially less working in a group or hospital, however you won't have marketing and overhead costs coming out of the fees.

WHERE DO I WORK?

A childbirth educator can choose to work for a hospital program, to affiliate with a birthing center or obstetrician's office, or to teach independently out of her home. To choose the best situation for you, consider whether you prefer to be affiliated with the medical community or independent of it, the opportunities that are available in your area, your need for either a steady flow of classes (and income) or the flexibility of teaching on your own schedule, and the situation for which your training prepares you. Consider also whether you prefer to focus just on teaching or if you also want the challenge of running a small business.

When exploring your options, check with your own obstetrician (and the obstetrician's nurse) for suggestions. Contact your local chapter of the International Childbirth Education Association (ICEA), the American Society for Psychoprophylaxis in Obstetrics/ Lamaze (ASPO/Lamaze), or other certifying bodies. They may even have a job placement service. Talk with childbirth educators in your community.

Teaching in a Hospital-based Program

Hospitals with maternity wards routinely host childbirth- and parenting-preparation series. They find it a useful way to attract young couples at the start of the family growth cycle. A good experience at a hospital could secure the family's business for a generation. Some educators report a conflict with the hospital's policies and their personal teaching preferences. For example, some hospitals require that an anesthesiologist guest lecture to each preparation class. As an educator, you may object to the assumption that all women will choose to use anesthesia. A benefit to holding classes at the hospital is that the pregnant woman becomes familiar with the surroundings and atmosphere, which should make her more likely to relax in labor.

Arlene's Career

Arlene Stach has been a childbirth educator for more than eighteen years. During that time, she has taught out of her home and with various area hospitals. She chose the career because she wanted to be home during the day to raise her four children, but she needed to work. The evening classes meant her husband could care for the children on the nights that she taught. Arlene's previous experience as a high school teacher was helpful. She also has an interest in nursing and found the process of birth and parenting fascinating.

In order to establish credibility, Arlene became certified by ASPO/Lamaze. At that time in her part of the country, it was the most prestigious of the certifying groups. It still has the best name recognition by consumers.

At the beginning of her career, Arlene chose to teach out of her home. It was convenient for her, and, at the time, childbirth education classes weren't usually affiliated with hospitals. Couples who wanted to prepare for childbirth had to seek out classes. However, there were drawbacks to teaching in her own home. She had to have enough room for all the couples to be able to both sit in chairs and to fit on the floor for the exercises. Her husband had to baby-sit and keep her young family quiet so as not to disturb or distract the class. She had to train her husband not to interrupt classes with a baby that refused to be comforted (though occasionally that was unavoidable). She was responsible for self-employment taxes. She had to pay for all her own class materials. She had to do her own marketing and promotion. She had to set fees and collect the money from the couples.

Currently Arlene teaches a total of five classes a week for two different hospitals. Many of her couples call her at home for advice before and after the baby is born. Part of why she enjoys her job is that ongoing contact with her clients. She still enjoys the classes, and each class is different; but over the past five years, she has started teaching classes in related fields such as grandparent classes and newborn care.

About 65 percent of all educators affiliate with either a hospital or a doctor's office. The hospital or doctor's office will probably require either that you are an RN or that you are certified by any of the major national or regional certifying groups, several of which are quite influential in their fields. Hospitals may prefer that you be group certified and may even pay for your certification.

Contact the director of patient education at hospitals where you would like to work, and find out if they require any specific certification and if they reimburse for training. Ask about what other classes the hospital offers to the public and if you would be considered as a teacher for those classes also. Discover what type of client they serve—perhaps you have a special skill that will help you, such as speaking Spanish fluently.

If You are Interested in Teaching in Birthing Centers

Birthing centers have a strong commitment to childbirth education because, most often, their focus is on avoidance of unnecessary drug intervention. If some of your reasons for wanting to be a childbirth educator include wanting to encourage women to have a more natural birth, avoiding interventions like fetal monitoring and drugs, this may be the best place for you to teach.

Contact the director of patient education, and find out if they require any specific certification and if they reimburse for training. Also ask about the type of clients they serve (in order to match your unique skills) and what other classes are offered.

Teaching Independently

This option gives you the most flexibility, the most potential for making money, and the least job security. As an independent educator, you run your own small business and handle marketing, bookkeeping, tax forms, scheduling, new class ideas/development, the purchase of class supplies, and the actual teaching. Your first step is to establish your credibility with local obstetricians so that they will recommend your classes to their patients (pregnant women nearly always go to the class recommended by their obstetrician). You can also attract clients by letting hospitals know of your availability; often their classes fill up and they need to refer pregnant women to other classes. Don't overlook advertising, promotion, and word of mouth. If you choose to be independent, you have to become an entrepreneur and run your program like a business. All the responsibility for scheduling classes, collecting fees, and filling the classes with pregnant women is yours. With the responsibility, you also gain the flexibility of working as many or as few hours as you like and teaching exactly what you choose, rather than teaching from another's syllabus.

TRAINING AND CERTIFICATION

There are no legal restrictions to calling yourself a childbirth educator—no required certification, license, or test. Nearly half of all childbirth educators are trained registered nurses, but most nurses who are educators have taken a break from nursing. As a practical matter, if you aren't an RN, you will find it much easier to get hired if you become certified by one of the major childbirth education organizations. The average educator teaches in a hospital-sponsored class two nights a week. About half of all educators are certified by ASPO/Lamaze (the official organization of Lamaze), ICEA, or a major regional group. (A complete listing of groups and associations for childbirth educators and educators in training can be found on pages 44–46.)

Of the 25,000 childbirth educators in the United States, about 35 percent are certified by ASPO/Lamaze; another 20 percent are certified by ICEA. There are several other regional certifying groups that have excellent reputations (see Resources at the end of the chapter). Before choosing which group to train with for certification, check with your local hospitals, doctors, and birthing centers to see which certification is favored in your area.

The certification process varies substantially from each organization. All require home study and attendance at training seminars. Most require student teaching with a senior educator. Several require the trainee to be present at an actual birth. Following is a discussion of three national certification programs. You can also explore regional programs that may be popular in your area (listed in Associations and Organizations for Childbirth Educators in Resources at the end of the chapter).

ASPO/Lamaze

The best known of all the groups, ASPO has been certifying childbirth educators for more than thirty years. The Lamaze method was developed in France by Dr. Ferdinand Lamaze and was popularized in the United States by Elisabeth Bing, founder of ASPO/Lamaze, in her book *Six Practical Lessons for an Easier Childbirth.* The book and the method encouraged women to approach childbirth as a shared event for both mother and father.

You can be a member of ASPO without being certified by them. ASPO teaches very specific breathing patterns and coping techniques for each stage of labor. The program emphasizes support by a partner to coach the laboring woman through contractions with focal points, patterned breathing, and muscle relaxation. They have just reviewed and changed their training requirements to shorten the time required and to make it university-based. ASPO has about 3,500 members and certifies a few hundred educators a year. They claim that about one-quarter of American women who give birth are taught by ASPO-certified childbirth educators (ACCE).

Requirements for ASPO certification: You must either be an RN, a physical therapist, or an occupational therapist *or* have a baccalaureate or higher degree from a recognized college or university, including successful completion of a supervised practicum, social work internship, or student teaching.

You must study (at home) four Study Guide modules: maternal/newborn care, the Lamaze method, the professional role of the childbirth educator, and instruction. You must attend a three- to four-day seminar sponsored by the program and taught by an ASPO-Lamaze faculty member, and you must observe a series of Lamaze classes and several births, develop a curriculum plan, and student-teach a Lamaze class series.

Upon completion of the program, you are then eligible to sit for the certification examination. The test is offered in April and in October each year. You are encouraged to maintain your certification by submitting 30 contact hours of approved continuing education every three years. (Contact hours are obtained by attending a seminar or by reading an approved article and successfully completing the quiz following; one contact hour roughly equals one seminar hour.)

ASPO sponsors an annual conference with continuing education seminars and opportunities for educators to network. The conference is open to all childbirth educators (not just ASPO-certified educators).

ICEA

This organization just started certifying educators five to ten years ago. Their program seems more popular because it is shorter and not as rigorous as ASPO's. Classes taught by ICEA-certified educators focus on family-centered maternity care. As an organization, ICEA supports the philosophy of freedom of choice based on knowledge of alternatives in maternity and newborn care. ICEA has not developed a unique brand name for their classes, like Lamaze. Rather the ICEA-certified educator will teach a class offering a variety of approaches to labor and delivery borrowing from methods such as Bradley, Read, and Lamaze. ICEA has nearly 8,000 members and certifies a few hundred educators a year. In total, ICEA has certified more than 1,900 educators. Membership in ICEA does not require that you be certified by them. About half of the members of ASPO are also members of ICEA. ICEA sponsors an annual conference with continuing education seminars and opportunities for educators to network. The conference is open to all childbirth educators. You do not need to be a member of ICEA to attend the conference.

ICEA's training program is called the "Teacher Certification Program" (TCP) and uses independent study to build on the background and skills you bring into the program. No specific background or education is required before starting to study for certification. Teaching skills are not included in the TCP. To start in the program, you must join ICEA and buy their study guides, which cover nearly all of the medical and psychological aspects of birth with which you will need to be familiar.

Requirements for ICEA certification: Observe a minimum of two labors and births, acquire a minimum of eighteen ICEA contact hours, and successfully complete an Evaluated Teaching Series. (Contact hours are obtained by attending a seminar or by reading an approved article and successfully completing the quiz following; one contact hour roughly equals one seminar hour.) Candidates must fulfill the requirements within a two-year period and must take and pass the certification examination within another year. The certification examination is given in April and in October in every state and also at the annual convention. Certified educators are allowed to use the letters ICCE (for ICEA Certified Childbirth Educator) after their name.

The costs involved are minimal and are spread out over two years. In 1996, the contact hours cost about $10 an hour, and the certification examination fee is $160. Scholarships are available for the certification examination and the cost of the convention.

Certified educators are encouraged to maintain their certification by a combination of contact hours, education workshops, labor/birth observations, or other options available.

The Bradley Method (previously known as Husband-Coached Childbirth)

Developed by Dr. Robert Bradley early in the 1960s, this method is enjoying a resurgence of popularity. The Bradley Method is taught in twelve classes starting early in pregnancy, rather than the shorter series of six, all in the last trimester, in most other programs. Because of the length of the course, Bradley courses cover a broad range of topics in more detail than most childbirth preparation classes can. There is a strong emphasis on having a natural—unmedicated—birthing experience, with additional focus on good nutrition in pregnancy and on breastfeeding.

Requirements for Bradley certification: A three-part training program consists of (1) an academic package, (2) the teacher workshop, and (3) the teaching of a provisional class series. The academic package includes book reports, outlines, and frequently asked questions that can be answered from the books. The candidate must prepare surveys of options and services available for parents in the community where she will teach. The four-day teacher workshop, limited to about twenty applicants per workshop, requires an application from the candidate and a deposit of $195 to attend. Only sixteen workshops are scheduled each year. After passing the test at the end of the workshop, the candidate becomes a provisional affiliate and may teach her first class series. She must send in weekly reports on her twelve-week series. A closed-book exam is mailed to the provisional affiliate after all the reports are in, and after passing, she becomes an affiliate. Annual reaffiliation fees are about $80.

There are other regional and national certifying organizations that have very good reputations. Check out the Resources at the end of this chapter, and get advice from practicing childbirth educators in your area before committing to a program.

WHAT SUPPLIES WILL I NEED?

Assuming that you have the educational background and are ready to start your first class, you will need a location with room for eight to fifteen couples to sit in chairs for part of the class and to spread out on the floor for the exercises. You will also need name tags, juice and cookies for the class break, and audio/visual support materials. If you're affiliated with a hospital or established program, a room and materials will probably all be supplied. If you are independent, you might be able to borrow some or all of the audio/visuals for a short time from fellow educators.

HOW DO I FIND CLIENTS?

If you are affiliated with a hospital or established program, finding clients will not be a problem. If you are an independent, obstetrician and hospital referrals are key. Don't overlook advertising, promotion, and word of mouth.

If you like to work with groups of highly motivated, happy people and if you love the birth process, then being a childbirth educator can be a rewarding career for you. Use the yellow pages to locate childbirth educators today, and ask them some questions!

TYPICAL FOUR-WEEK CLASS OUTLINE

This is the outline of a typical hospital-based series of childbirth classes. Most of the exercises and pain-coping techniques taught are Lamaze-based, but the information would be included in any class. A series typically runs no less than four weeks and no more than six weeks. The series would have the same amount of teaching hours—two hours a week for six weeks or three hours a week for four weeks.

CLASS ONE

I. Introduction of couples

A. Names

B. Background

C. Due date

D. What they want to learn from class

II. Course particulars

A. Length of classes and course

B. How couples will be expected to participate

C. Content of classes

III. Video: "Hello Baby" (about 25 minutes)

IV. What is "childbirth preparation"?—*Many couples take the class because they are told to by their obstetricians. Now is the time to sell them on the class so they will participate and benefit fully.*

V. The role of the coach—*Demystify the "coach," and reassure the coaches that they won't be called on to do* *anything they are uncomfortable doing and that they won't faint at the birth!*

VI. Relaxation

A. A discussion of the role of relaxation in labor but also in late pregnancy

B. Introduction of first breathing pattern

VII. Discomforts and body changes during pregnancy

A. Backache

B. Clumsy sex

C. Linea nigra

D. Mask of pregnancy

E. Hemorrhoids/constipation

F. Swelling

G. Weight gain

VIII. Preterm labor

A. Signs and medical indications of preterm labor

B. What your health care provider might do to prevent it or stop it

C. What interventions can be expected, including bed rest

IX. Early labor management

A. Early signs of labor

B. Calling the doctor/midwife

C. Suggested activities (eating lightly, drinking water, walking)

X. **Neuromuscular relaxation**—*Focal point: facilitates outward focus, keeping the woman calm in labor*

CLASS TWO

I. **Tour of obstetrics floor (slides and walk through)**—*Encouraged even in non-hospital-based courses because seeing the labor floor before she is in labor helps her visualize labor. Feeling familiar with her surroundings increases a woman's ability to relax and helps make her feel more in control.*

II. **Fetal monitoring**

A. Required at various stages of labor in most hospitals

B. Women need to know what level of monitoring is necessary and their options about limiting monitoring.

III. **Active labor management**

A. Signs and symptoms of active labor

B. Coping skills

C. Comfort skills for the coach to use

D. Possible interventions

IV. **Back labor**

A. Definition and description

B. Pain-coping techniques

V. **Relaxation—Role it plays in labor**

VI. Review of first breathing pattern and effleurage

VII. Second breathing pattern

VIII. Hyperventilation—Dangers and prevention

CLASS THREE

I. Film: "Having Your Baby by Cesarean" (10 minutes)

II. Cesarean birth discussion

A. Indications

B. Avoidance

C. Emotional response

D. VBAC (vaginal birth after cesarean)

III. Induction

A. Indications

B. What will happen

C. Drugs that will be used

D. Drugs' effect on mother and baby

IV. Analgesia and anesthesia

A. Continuous epidermal

B. Duramorph

C. General anesthesia

D. Local anesthesia—Role of the anesthesiologist

V. Relaxation

VI. Review of first and second breathing patterns

VII. Third breathing pattern

VIII. Transition

A. Definition and description

B. Signs and symptoms

C. Emotional reactions

D. Coping skills

E. Comfort techniques for the coach

F. Hospital procedures

IX. Premature urge to push

A. Reason it impedes delivery

B. Techniques to resist the urge to push

CLASS FOUR

I. Film: "Labor and Delivery—Have a Healthy Baby" (60 minutes)

II. Pushing

A. What it feels like

B. Do's and don't's

C. Time frame

III. Delivery room

A. Episiotomy

B. Interventions

C. Afterbirth

D. Apgar score

E. Appearance of the baby

F. What the staff will do to the baby

IV. Recovery room

A. Time

B. Emotions

C. Exhaustion

D. Postdelivery high

V. Relaxation

VI. Review of breathing patterns

VII. Fears and concerns—General class discussion

RESOURCES

ASSOCIATIONS AND ORGANIZATIONS FOR CHILDBIRTH EDUCATORS

American Society of Psychoprophylaxis in Obstetrics, Inc. (ASPO/Lamaze)
ASPO/Lamaze
1200 19th Street, NW
Suite 300
Washington, DC 20036-2422
202-857-1128
e-mail: ASPO@SBA.com
ASPO offers certification and continuing education for childbirth educators. It is also branching out to offer certification in related fields such as lactation consultation and doula services.

American Academy of Husband Coached Childbirth
aka The Bradley Method
Box 5224
Sherman Oaks, CA 91413-5224
800-4A-BIRTH
World Wide Web site: http://www.bradleybirth.com
The Bradley Method's goal is to teach parents how to give birth without medication.

Association of Labor Assistants and Childbirth Educators (ALACE)
P.O. Box 382724
Cambridge, MA 02238
617-441-2500
World Wide Web site: http://www.alace.org
They are a relatively new organization and have a large, very informative web site.

Birth Support Providers, International
3941 Park Drive #20-114
El Dorado Hills, CA 95762
916-974-8143

Council of Childbirth Education Specialists
8 Sylvan Glen
East Lyme, CT 06333
860-739-9176

C/SEC International
(Cesarean Support Education & Concern)
22 Forest Road
Framingham, MA 01701
508-877-8266
As its name implies, the focus is on cesarean prevention and education.

Informed Home Birth/Informed Home Parenting
P.O. Box 3675
Ann Arbor, MI 48106
313-662-6857

International Childbirth Educator Association (ICEA)
P.O. Box 20048
Minneapolis, MN 55420
612-854-8660
ICEA also offers certification and continuing education. Their teaching program is generally considered to offer more flexibility for the teacher.

Read Natural Childbirth Foundation
P.O. Box 150956
San Rafael, CA 94915
415-456-8462

Founded by Dr. Grantly Dick-Read in the 1940s to teach the pain-coping techniques that emphasize body awareness, deep muscle relaxation, and breathing methods.

SUPPLIES AND CATALOGS

Childbirth Graphics
P.O. Box 21207
Waco, TX 76702-1207
800-299-3366
World Wide Web site: http://www.wrsgroup.com
A complete catalog of teaching aids for birth, sex, and parenting education.

Cradle Publishing, Inc.
Childbirth Instructor Magazine
124 East 40th Street, 1101
New York, NY 10016
212-986-1422
Order *Childbirth Instructor Magazine* for $17.95; quarterly plus a special issue each year. Published in association with *Baby Magazine* and *Baby Magazine's Infant Care Guide*.

LifeCircle
Marjorie M. Pyle
2378 Cornell Drive
Costa Mesa, CA 92626
A variety of videos, booklets, and slides for childbirth and parenting education.

Polymorph Films
118 South Street
Boston, MA 02111
800-223-5107
Videotapes and films on childbirth and pregnancy issues.

Vida Health Communications
6 Bigelow Street
Cambridge, MA 02139
617-864-4334
Birthing videos.

BOOKS

Teaching Natural Birth by Jan Witcome. San Diego, CA: Thornwood Gardens Publishing Company.

Emphasis on the Bradley Method, but good marketing information for all educators and aspiring educators. $21.95 (California tax applies) check or money order. To order, call 619-287-4479, or write to publisher at P.O. Box 152072, San Diego, CA 92195.

Childbirth Education: Practice, Research, and Theory by Francine H. Nichols and Sharron Smith Humenick. Philadelphia: W. B. Saunders Company, 1988.

3

PREPARING WOMEN FOR THE MARATHON OF THEIR LIVES: MATERNITY FITNESS INSTRUCTOR

What will you do?	Help women prepare for "the marathon of labor"
How many hours a week?	3–20 one-hour classes
Your work hours?	Variable; usually evenings and weekends
Will you need licensing/ certification?	None required, but recommended
What can you earn?	$10–$15 per student per class
Liability insurance needed?	None required; employers may supply

No one would run a marathon without training. Then why do so many women fail to prepare for what maternal fitness instructor Julie Tupler terms "the marathon of labor"?

The fact is that many women don't realize the physical stamina it takes to make it through nine months of pregnancy, then labor and delivery, followed possibly by a postpartum series of sleepless marathons with baby. Help to spread the word. If you're a social person who is interested (and, preferably, trained) in fitness—perhaps a former physical education teacher or physical therapist, or perhaps just a fitness enthusiast—and if you're interested in helping pregnant women stay fit throughout pregnancy, here's an opportunity for you: become a maternity fitness instructor!

WHY THE NEED?

Everyone who exercises regularly knows what keeps you exercising: you feel better. The health benefits, while undeniable, are not as compelling as that high that follows a good workout. For the expectant mom, however, the benefits of exercise are more compelling.

Studies show that women who exercise have a lower cesarean-section rate, shorter labor, and fewer low-birthweight babies: a 1990 study showed that women who exercised during pregnancy had a 30 percent shorter labor and fewer obstetric interventions, such as forceps and cesarean section. A 1995 study found that women who continued regular aerobic activity throughout pregnancy averaged smaller weight gains and accumulated less body fat—benefits that will certainly give a woman the upper hand in the postpartum battle of the bulge.

IN A "DELICATE CONDITION"?

Hardly. Gone are the days when the expectant mom was not to lift anything heavy, not to stay on her feet, not to reach over her head, and not to run—except in the most dire emergency. Pregnancy may not be the time to start a rigorous exercise program, but a healthy woman with a healthy pregnancy can and should continue a regular exercise program.

However, pregnancy does result in complex physiologic changes, and special precautions are needed to ensure an exercise program that is safe and beneficial for the expectant mom. Among the physical changes that occur with pregnancy are the following:

Lungs and breathing

In pregnancy, the respiratory rate is naturally increased. Because of this, the body works harder to supply enough oxygen to the developing fetus. This can reduce the amount of oxygen available for exercise and can cause decreased endurance and a sense of breathlessness.

Muscles and skeleton

Because of the enlarging womb, the lower back develops more curvature and the center of gravity shifts. This changes a woman's sense of balance and requires adjustments in posture to prevent injury. Usually, women find that they naturally alter their exercise program to accommodate these changes, especially in the last trimester of pregnancy.

The joints also undergo changes during pregnancy. The body releases the hormone *relaxin*, which loosens up the joints of the pelvis to make room for the birth of the child. Because all of the joints in the body are more lax, there is a greater chance of spraining or straining muscles and joints during pregnancy.

Metabolism

The expectant mother's body uses carbohydrates more quickly. Exercise further increases the metabolism of carbohydrates. These two factors can lead to low blood sugar reactions during exercise. Increasing caloric intake (by 200 to 300 calories per day) to shift the carbohydrate balance is very important for pregnant exercisers.

Heart and blood vessels

The expectant mother's body increases its blood volume by 40 percent over the prepregnancy level. Heart rate increases by about fifteen beats per minute. This allows nutrients and oxygen to be transported to the fetus more efficiently. However, with the growth of the womb, the flow of blood in the body can be disrupted, causing lightheadedness.

HOW EXERCISE AFFECTS PREGNANCY, AND HOW PREGNANCY SHOULD AFFECT EXERCISE

Typically, women exercise to burn calories and to lose body fat. But when a woman is pregnant, she needs to gain weight to assure a healthy pregnancy. Therefore, exercise goals need to be modified. Other physiologic changes take place that will affect *how* a woman exercises during pregnancy.

During exercise, blood flow shifts away from the internal organs so that muscles, lungs, and heart get a larger share of oxygen. Extremely vigorous exercise can cause too large a shift of oxygen away from the uterus; thus, strenuous exercise is not recommended during pregnancy.

During exercise, the brain releases *norepinephrine*, a neurotransmitter that can reduce depression and influence blood flow to the heart and kidneys. Norepinephrine also increases smooth muscle contractions, and causes increased uterine activity in the form of painless contractions. These contractions have not been shown to cause labor, but women who are at risk for preterm labor should engage in only mild exercise.

Finally, exercise causes an increase in core body temperature.

Commonly Asked Questions about Exercise during Pregnancy

Here are some questions you're likely to hear from prospective clients.

• *I've never had a regular exercise program. Is it safe to start one now?*

Pregnancy is not the time to begin an exercise program. However, even a regular half hour of walking or stretching can be beneficial. Do not begin any new exercise program without consulting your health care provider.

• *How will exercise affect my developing baby?*

All of the effects of exercise on the fetus are not well understood. However, moderate (not vigorous) exercise in a cool environment may, in fact, be beneficial to both mother and baby. More vigorous exercise, some experts say, can lead to potentially harmful changes in fetal heart rate. With intense exercise, the fetus may be affected by rises in maternal temperature.

• *How long should I exercise?*

Start out with a short routine, lasting about fifteen minutes, and gradually increase it. Keep your pulse rate below 140 beats per minute. And whenever you exercise, drink lots of fluids.

• *Are there women who should not exercise during pregnancy?*

Yes. Exercise only on the advice of your health care professional if you have any of the following conditions: pregnancy-induced high blood pressure, ruptured membranes, weak cervix, persistent second- and third-trimester bleeding, preterm labor in this or a previous pregnancy, slow fetal growth, and certain chronic diseases such as asthma and diabetes.

Some studies show that high fevers during the first three months of pregnancy can affect fetal development; other studies have not confirmed these findings. However, extremely fit women actually have improved body-temperature regulation and have a decreased core body temperature during pregnancy. Because of the conflicting data, general guidelines are to exercise with caution in very hot weather and to drink plenty of fluids during exercise classes.

WHAT DOES A PREGNANCY EXERCISE CLASS OFFER?

It can be an hour of exercise, or it can be more comprehensive. Julie Tupler, a childbirth educator, fitness instructor, and personal trainer in New York City, developed Maternal Fitness, a program geared toward exercise, nutrition, stress management, and the physical and psychological preparation for labor. She realized that women have different fitness needs during pregnancy. The Maternal Fitness program is, she says, for everybody, no matter what their fitness level or stage of pregnancy. She hopes to get women involved in the Maternal Fitness program early in their pregnancies to prepare both their bodies and their minds. Her program is taught by registered nurses who are also certified personal trainers and who have gone through an intensive Maternal Fitness Training program.

Tupler is author of the book *Maternal Fitness*. This step-by-step book on keeping fit during pregnancy is an excellent resource if you're interested in becoming a pregnancy exercise instructor. Tupler has an exercise/pregnancy health video as well, "Coming Contractions."

Ann Cowlin developed Dancing Thru Pregnancy, a variation on the classic exercise program in that it is based on principles of dance, exercise physiology, and group support. She approaches each class as a choreographic challenge. Like other programs, it is designed to ease the discomforts of pregnancy and to provide skills for labor. After delivery, Cowlin encourages her clients to continue with After Dance, a workout program designed for both mother and infant. All of the instructors in this program are trained in physical education, exercise physiology, dance, or childbirth education.

Dancing Thru Pregnancy, claims Cowlin, actually produces measurable results. During 1992, the cesarean delivery rate at Yale New Haven Hospital (the program connected with Dancing Thru Pregnancy) was 4 percent, compared with the overall hospital rate of 18 percent. An independent study done in 1991 placed the combined forceps and extraction rate at less than 6 percent.

Nationally, the YMCA has been teaching exercise programs for pregnant women since 1983. The first national program, You and Me, Baby, was developed by Susan Regnier and the St. Paul, Minnesota, YMCA and became the model for all YMCAs nationally. The updated program now taught at YMCAs across the country offers guided exercise and educational classes for women who want to improve their overall health and fitness.

Motherwell classes, part of a national program developed by fitness instructor Bonnie Berk in Carlisle, Pennsylvania, involve at least one hour of exercise that includes warm-up, cardiovascular workout, floor work, weight training, flexibility, posture, and coordination. Self-pacing techniques are incorporated throughout so women can exercise at their own comfort and tolerance levels and at all stages of pregnancy. Also included are five-minute discussion topics on nutrition, body mechanics, stress management, and issues related specifically to the pregnancy and postpartum experience. The Motherwell program is available through businesses, health maintenance organizations (HMOs), and health clubs.

One-on-one maternal fitness training is another option. In this case, the fitness instructor becomes a personal trainer. This type of program is very popular in upscale populations for fitness buffs who may have a tight schedule and don't want to go to a gym—but they don't want to give up fitness.

These are but a few examples of the types of classes you could develop. These programs do, however, have one thing in common: they strive to be fun for every participant while offering enough of a challenge to keep the mom-to-be in shape. Every workout session begins with an adequate warm-up period (five to seven minutes). The main portion of the session is aerobic activity—walking, jogging (if comfortable), biking, swimming, tennis, or low-impact or step aerobics—which should last twenty to thirty minutes to maximize the benefits to the cardiovascular system. This should be followed by a cool-down period (at least five minutes). Water should be available to participants throughout.

TRAINING AND CERTIFICATION

Certification is not required, but it is highly recommended, both for your own knowledge and for your client's safety. Many certifying programs are available for exercise instructors, although not all of them have certification for maternity fitness. Bonnie Berk developed the Motherwell training program exclusively for maternity health-and-fitness programs. Motherwell program packages are available through a turnkey licensure system that will provide everything you need to offer a safe maternity health-and-fitness program. Packages include instructor training as well as training materials and camera-ready artwork to help you make your own brochures and posters.

Motherwell also offers a "Train the Trainer" program so that those trained in the program can train additional instructors. Training covers all aspects of program management, including proven promotional strategies and, again, artwork for brochures and posters. Motherwell offers its Land certification at its headquarters in Carlisle, Pennsylvania, and a Home-Study course; training for Water Fitness Instructor certification is offered only at the company headquarters.

Among the variety of professional organizations that certify exercise instructors, one of the most popular is the American Council on Exercise (ACE) (see Resources at the end of the chapter). ACE, established in 1985, offers certification programs for aerobics instructors, personal trainers, and lifestyle and weight-management consultants and provides a variety of health and fitness education services to the public.

WHAT'S THE FIRST STEP?

Look into programs described in the preceding section. Are they available in your area? Can you get training in them? Then, unless you're planning on becoming a personal trainer in a client's home, you'll first have to investigate available facilities. Contact local health clubs, YMCAs and YWCAs, and medical centers. Find out about programs for pregnancy fitness. Find out what they charge, what training is required for the instructor, and what facilities are available. Although exercise instructors need not be licensed in many areas, many clubs may have requirements of their own staff. What are those requirements? If a health club doesn't have pregnancy fitness classes, offer your services.

WHERE DO I WORK?

Your space need not be in a gym; a church basement or a community center may serve your needs. Be sure to instruct clients to wear comfortable clothing and to bring along a mat for floor work.

Are there community pools? Swimming may be a great exercise early in pregnancy. Find out if you can reserve an hour for pregnancy swims. Ask if you can rent space for pregnancy exercise classes.

If you become a personal trainer and go to the expectant mom's home, be sure that she has lots of space for floor work. She must have a clean space without too many distractions—such as older children, a housekeeper, or pets. Mats are a must.

WHAT WILL I BE TEACHING?

First and foremost, safety must be stressed. The American College of Obstetrics and Gynecology (ACOG) recommends the following guidelines for exercise during pregnancy:

- Regular exercise, at least three times a week, is preferable to sporadic activity. If you cannot get clients in three times a week, encourage them to exercise between classes.
- Exercise in the supine (back-lying) position should be avoided after the first three months of pregnancy.
- A pregnant woman should listen to her body while exercising. If something is painful or causes dizziness and faintness, the woman should stop.
- A pregnant woman should not exercise to the point of exhaustion.
- An instructor should be aware of the pregnant woman's changing center of gravity and should not encourage exercise involving the potential for even mild abdominal trauma.
- Plenty of water should be drunk before, during, and after exercise classes to regulate the woman's body temperature and that of the baby.
- After delivery, a woman can resume prepregnancy exercise routines gradually; many of the physical changes of pregnancy persist for four to six weeks after delivery.

Exercise instructors, for their own legal protection and for the welfare of their clients, should distribute these guidelines to their clients—they encourage good sense and safety as well as comfort.

The workout should include strength training exercises for both the upper and lower body, using light hand weights or resistance tubing. Abdominal exercises should be a part of the routine, but the back-lying position should be avoided after the first three months of pregnancy. The abdominals can be worked in a side-lying, quadruped (on forearms and knees), or sitting position by exhaling as the abdominals contract and inhaling as they are released.

Pelvic floor exercises are very important. The pelvic floor is a sling of muscles that supports many internal organs (uterus, bladder, and kidneys). As pregnancy progresses, the uterus exerts more and more pressure on the pelvic floor and can cause it to collapse if it is not kept strong. If the pelvic floor collapses, the result may be problems such as urinary incontinence or uterine prolapse.

To keep the pelvic floor, or Kegel muscles, strong and to make exercising easier, the Kegel exercise should be encouraged as a daily routine for pregnant (and nonpregnant!) women. The exercises will also help the uterus contract back down to normal size after birth.

One of the most common complaints of pregnant women is back pain. Strengthening the back muscles can prevent injury during delivery and help lessen aches and pains during pregnancy. Remind your clients that it's also important to pay attention to posture. Keep the head erect, the shoulders back, and the pelvis tilted forward when standing or walking.

Always end the workout session with a full body stretch to avoid muscle tightness and soreness the next day. Each stretch should be held for twenty to thirty seconds. Avoid ballistic or bouncing movements to reduce joint stress. During each session, be sure to keep water available.

HOW DO I FIND CLIENTS?

The earlier in pregnancy you find your clients, the better, not just for reasons of their health, but also because they will be your maternity-fitness clients for a longer time. Focus on reaching women as soon as they find that they're pregnant. If you get a job with a health club, a Y, or a community organization, take an active part in promoting the class. If you plan to offer classes on your own, prepare informational brochures about exercise during pregnancy, allowing enough space to advertise your services. For example, you might reproduce the ACOG Guidelines for Exercise during Pregnancy, putting your name, phone number, and a class schedule at the bottom. Prepare a flier of commonly asked questions about exercise during pregnancy (see page 54). Give fliers to health care providers in your area, such as local clinics, nurse-midwives, physicians, and managed care organizations. Also go to local health clubs, which, if they don't offer maternity fitness classes, may be willing to refer clients. And, as always, remember that word of mouth can be your best advertisement. Those who have enjoyed your classes may encourage their friends to join them.

HOW MUCH DO I CHARGE?

If you work in a health club, the price of membership likely includes maternity fitness classes, and you'll receive a salary from the club. If you're planning your own exercise classes, women will expect to pay $10 to $15 per class. When deciding how much to charge, keep in mind the cost of space rental, if applicable.

To encourage women to return for your classes (and they should be encouraged to have an exercise session at least three times per week), you could sell exercise-class coupon booklets that incorporate a discount for several classes. For example, a single class might be available for $15; a ten-class coupon booklet could cost $100 to $120.

For personal training sessions, charge $35 to $50 per session; in some areas, you may be able to charge more. Contact local exercise facilities to find out what the going rate is.

What a great way to earn money! Being a maternity fitness instructor will help you keep in shape as you help pregnant women keep in shape as their bodies change and grow. Whether you decide to go into business for yourself or offer your services to a local health club, a career in maternity fitness is an opportunity to meet people, to provide a worthwhile service, and maybe to start a new business.

SUGGESTED EXERCISE CLASS OUTLINE

I. Discussion/sharing (5–10 minutes)—Potential topics:

A. Correct posture

B. ACOG guidelines

C. Danger signs in pregnancy/postpartum

D. Safe sports activities

II. Warm up (5–10 minutes)

A. Heel steps

B. Knee bends

C. Walking in place

D. Low forward kicks

E. Slow arm movements

III. Stretching (5–10 minutes)

A. Hamstring/calf stretches

B. Upper back stretch

C. Cat backs

D. Pectoral stretch

IV. Light aerobics (20–30 minutes)

A. Direction marching

B. Heel steps

C. Kick backs (hamstring)

D. Knee lifts

E. Arm movements

Bicep curls

Tricep reaches

Shoulder rolls

Butterfly arms

Pulldowns

Lateral raises

V. Strengthening/toning (15 minutes)

A. Upper leg raises

B. Lower leg lifts

C. Bent knee lifts

D. Ankle circles

E. Modified pushups

F. Pelvic rocks

G. Back strengthening

H. Kegels

VI. Relaxation

A. Progressive relaxation

B. Imagery

C. Quiet response

RESOURCES

BOOKS

Exercise in Pregnancy, edited by R. Artal-Mittelmark, R. Wiswell, and B. Drinkwater. Baltimore: Williams & Wilkins, 1991.

The Bodywise Woman by Judy Makle Lutter, Lynne Jaffee. Champaign, IL: Human Kinetics, 1996.

Maternal Fitness: Preparing for the Marathon of Labor by Julie Tupler. New York: Fireside, 1996.

VIDEOTAPES

"Fit for Two—The Official YMCA Prenatal Exercise Guide" by YMCA of the USA with Thomas W. Hanlon. $13.95 through Human Kinetics, 1607 Market Street, Champaign, IL 61820; phone 800-747-4457.

"The Motherwell Home Exercise Video." Available through mail order only, 800-MOMWELL.

CERTIFYING ORGANIZATIONS

Motherwell Program Packages
800-MOMWELL
Motherwell program packages are available through a turnkey licensure system. You will receive everything you need to offer a successful, medically proven maternity-health-and-fitness program that follows the safety guidelines of the American College of Obstetricians and Gynecologists.

American Council on Exercise (ACE)
5820 Oberline Drive
Suite 102
San Diego, CA 92121-3787
800-825-3636 or 619-535-8227
World Wide Web site: http://www.acefitness.org

American Fitness Professionals & Associates
P.O. Box 214
Ship Bottom, NJ 09009
800-494-7782
World Wide Web site: http://www.AFPA@fitness.com
An accredited certification agency that conducts continuing education conferences and seminars. Its web site offers a complete list of certifying organizations for fitness instructors.

4

SUPPORTING WOMEN DURING LABOR: THE DOULA

What will you do?	Provide labor support
How many hours a week?	Completely variable, depending on your client's labor
Your work hours?	Not traditional
Will you need licensing/ certification?	None required, but available
What can you earn?	$200–$800 per labor
Liability insurance needed?	No personal insurance required

Few events in the life of a couple bring them together as do the labor and delivery of a baby. Having the support of a doula can benefit both of the parents and can help ensure a positive birth experience.

THE DOULA'S ROLE

Doula, *birth assistant*, and *labor assistant* are nearly interchangeable terms. *Doula* is Greek for "in service of." The doula stays by the side of the laboring woman encouraging, comforting, supporting. She provides information and explanations before and during labor. Doulas and labor assistants do not provide medical or clinical skills; they don't make decisions for the mother; they don't take the place of an obstetrician or a midwife. They are there to nurture the mother—to mother the mother—and to be her health advocate within the hospital.

The services of doulas have only recently become widely available in the United States—so recently, in fact, that there remains some confusion over the term *doula*. Some professionals use it to indicate a *birth assistant* only; some feel the term and the job include (or can be used exclusively for) *postnatal, at-home support*. Doulas of North America (DONA), the major certifying organization, has decided to limit the term to mean "labor supporter" and to refer to professionals who work in the woman's home after the birth of the baby as *home doulas*. We will follow their lead.

As a birth assistant you are hired by the mother to work with her and her partner before labor to prepare her birth plan, during early labor before it is time to call in her health care professional, throughout labor, and for a limited amount after birth helping her establish breastfeeding and giving her a written record of the birth.

Women who choose to become doulas (I have heard of only one male doula) must be supportive and caring. Often a woman who is attracted to becoming a doula had a wonderful birth experience herself and wants to pass that experience along. Doulas often speak of birth as being "empowering," allowing women who have experienced a positive labor and delivery to have more confidence in themselves and in all aspects of their lives, especially parenting. Ironically, other women become doulas because they had a negative birth experience—not that it necessarily ended in cesarean section or other unexpected outcome, but that it left them feeling that the birth experience should be different. These women often make wonderful doulas. Most doulas have given birth themselves; however, this is not a requirement.

As a doula, you must be available to go to your client whenever she goes into labor. You must be fully available and undistracted for the entire time of labor. Your own family must be able to get along without you (perhaps not even a phone call), for a day or two at a time. Birth assisting is a physically and emotionally exhausting job. Often labor takes eighteen to twenty-four hours (average for a first labor), and you will be by the mother's side the entire time. Your personal life must not intrude; the birth takes priority.

Marshall Klaus, the doctor who coined the term *bonding*, published *Mothering the Mother: How a Doula Can Help You Have a Shorter and Healthier Birth* in 1993 releasing research about the benefits of a doula attending a birth. This was the first widely circulated work on doulas, and the conclusions his research drew give solid rationale for engaging a doula. He found that when a doula was present for the labor and delivery, women experienced:

- 50 percent reduction in the cesarean rate
- 25 percent shorter labor
- 60 percent reduction in epidural requests
- 40 percent reduction in oxytocin use
- 30 percent reduction in analgesia use
- 40 percent reduction in forceps delivery

This and other research studies illustrate clearly that doulas lower the average cost of birth. Presently most couples who choose to hire a doula pay for her services out of their own pockets. As insurance companies are becoming more aware of the health and financial benefits of doulas, more insurance companies and HMOs are reimbursing couples for the cost of the doula. The insurance company lowers the cost of birth, couples have a more satisfactory birth experience. Everybody wins with a doula.

THE DIFFERENCE BETWEEN A DOULA AND A LABOR COACH

If you become a doula, you may often be asked how your job differs from that of the labor coach. In childbirth education classes, the husband/partner is taught how to be the woman's primary labor support, her coach. However, watching the laboring woman experience pain, fatigue, or fear can be emotionally difficult and can make the coach forget all he or she learned in childbirth preparation classes. Dealing with his or her own feelings and emotions approaching birth, the coach may not be able to fully support the mother. The doula is there to support both the mother and father. The doula takes the stress of primary support off the coach if he is overwhelmed. In many labors, the doula is the only one of the three who has gone through labor before.

Because of the doula's experience, she can reassure the mother that what she is feeling is normal and that the labor is progressing. Also she is more fully trained than a coach is in labor support and will have a broader range of comforting techniques. Sometimes doulas give primary support to the mother, with the father or other support person nearby. If the father is uncertain of what to do, the doula can draw him by giving him small tasks. Other times the father will give the primary support, and the doula will stand by to offer reassurance and to suggest options. Rather than take over the birth experience, the doula works with the couple, allowing the father or partner to participate as fully as is comfortable, while making sure the mother's needs are being met.

HOW DO I FIND CLIENTS?

Most doulas work independently and depend on referrals, on word of mouth, and on advertising for new clients. It is customary for a woman hiring a doula to interview several before making a decision. Hopefully, the woman has already received a recommendation for you because she called you. However, she will probably ask for references during the interview. Be prepared with a short list of recent clients. If you are just starting out, prepare a list of mothers with whom you worked as an apprentice doula and a list of several doulas who will confirm that you are competent.

During the interview, be prepared to answer the following questions:

What services do you provide—
before birth?
during birth?
after birth?
What is your training and educational background?
How many births have you attended as a doula?
How long have you been a doula?
Are you certified as a doula?
Are you maintaining your certification through continuing education courses?
Are you familiar with the method of childbirth preparation in which the pregnant woman took classes?
What is your philosophy of birth?
Have you had children (experienced childbirth)?
Are there procedures to which you are ethically/intellectually opposed?
Have you attended births at the hospital/facility where she will give birth?
Have you attended a birth with her caregiver before?
Do you have a backup?

SERVICES OFFERED

Preparing the Couple for Birth

After you are hired, you will meet with the woman and her partner several times before the birth (if you have been hired enough in advance). The meetings are an opportunity for you to get to know the woman before labor, and to explore what her preparations have been for labor and delivery. Virtually all first-time mothers attend childbirth education classes—yet she still may have questions. A second-time mother (or multipara) might need to review pain-coping techniques. It's important to learn at this time (if you didn't discover this in the interview) why she is hiring a doula. Perhaps she was unhappy with a previous birth experience or is afraid of a cesarean. With this knowledge, you will be much better prepared to help her in labor. If there are any complications with the pregnancy, such as gestational diabetes, you may want to prepare yourself by some extra study.

You will also want to observe the relationship between the mother and the person whom she has chosen for her coach. Are they comfortable together? Does the mother speak frankly to and in front of the coach (implying trust)? Can you speak frankly to the coach and discuss how you will work together to support and encourage the woman? Now is a good time to find out if the coach feels threatened or if he or she will be able to work well with you.

The Birth Plan

Before labor starts, you will want to help the couple write a *birth plan*. The birth plan is very important. In preparing it, the pregnant woman and her partner explore their visions of what the birth will be like. Then they can record their preferences before the stresses of labor. For example, the birth plan should take into account procedures such as continuous fetal monitoring or episiotomies. Both procedures are standard in many hospitals but are controversial among doulas, monitrices, and midwives. You would make sure that the mother is well informed about both the benefits of the procedures and the negative repercussions each can have. You should discuss alternatives to each and should encourage her to discuss the procedures with her health care provider if she is considering avoiding them. Whether or not she chooses to list them in her birth plan as procedures to be avoided, you must support her decision regardless of your preferences. You are to provide information that allows the woman to give her own informed consent, and she has the right to do this without being judged by you.

Informed Consent

Regardless of preparation and training, some labors have an unexpected outcome. It may be minor—the woman choosing to request pain medication; or it may be monumental—the death of the infant. At every step, you make certain that the mother understands what is happening and what her options are. Her informed consent must be obtained before any procedure. Here are some questions to which the mother should know the answer before she can give informed consent:

- Why is this drug or procedure necessary?
- Will the baby and the mother be healthier for taking it or having it done? Is this routine?
- What are the known side effects?
- Will the benefits outweigh the side effects (in the mother's opinion)?
- What is the risk to both mother and baby if the procedure/drug is not given?
- Are there alternatives to try before the procedure/drug?

Labor Support

The mother will call you when she thinks she is in early labor, and you can help her determine if she is, indeed, in labor. Depending on your agreement, you can go to her immediately and work with her through early labor, which can take hours or even a couple of days, or you can wait and meet her at the hospital later in labor. As labor progresses, your primary job is to make sure the laboring woman's needs are being met. You also extend support and reassurance to the coach. After attending a number of births, you will have developed quite a large repertoire of laboring techniques and comfort measures, the doula's "bag of tricks." Even an inexperienced doula can fulfill the essential requirements of birth assistance: being there in every sense for the laboring woman.

Claudia Lowe, NACA, BSPI, describes three categories of labor support: adjunctive, needs-specific, and interventive. With your understanding of your client and her labor goals, these can help you gauge the level of support you need to be giving in labor.

- Certain *adjunctive* techniques are used to bring out the mother's own resources and to help her trust her body: Verbal encouragement, eye contact, brow wiping, and suggestions about changing positions are all measures that send the message "You're okay." About 70 to 80 percent of your comfort measures are adjunctive.
- *Needs-specific* techniques focus on specific situations such as back labor, failure to progress, and posterior presentation. About 10 to 20 percent of your comfort measures are needs-specific.
- *Interventive* techniques are used to forestall or avoid medical intervention. Squatting instead of forceps and nipple stimulation rather than Pitocin are two examples. These techniques are used when the mother and the health care provider are in agreement. About 5 to 10 percent of your comfort measures are interventive.

As a doula you do not perform medical or clinical tasks: You do not take blood pressure, you do not interpret fetal monitoring tapes, you do not check fetal heart rates. You should be familiar with all the standard medical procedures as well as all possible drug and procedural interventions so that you can help the caregiver explain them to the mother. You may be called upon to:

- Outline the reasons for the procedures
- Inform her of side effects or effects to her labor
- Let her know what may happen if she refuses the procedure
- Help the couple reach informed consent.

Much of this you would have discussed in your prenatal meeting; and if she was considering refusing any of the procedures, it would be mentioned in her birth plan.

While a doula is an advocate for the couple, you do not speak on their behalf. In the stress of labor, some women forget their birth plan and abandon their right to make decisions. You can remind her of her goals; and if changes have to be made in the birth plan, you can help her adjust. You enhance communication between the couple and their caregiver, perhaps asking questions that you believe will further clarify their options.

As labor progresses, you will work with the mother, applying the comfort techniques that you practiced in previous meetings. You'll use various breathing patterns, different body positions, showers, massage, Jacuzzi, cold cloths, touching/cradling her, walking, effleurage. All the while you'll encourage her, reminding her that her body knows what to do and that she should allow her body to take control. You'll let her know how well she is progressing and how close she is to finally having the baby she wants so much. The woman's partner may be very involved at this point or may choose to hang back a bit. Don't forget to offer encouragement and support to the partner—birth is difficult for him, too. If he is hanging back a bit, you'll want to ask him to do small things that are helpful, getting ice chips for example. Reassure him that, whatever he is doing, his being there is helping the mother.

Throughout labor you will need to respond to the laboring mother's changing needs. The light massage so welcome a few moments ago may be angrily rejected. A shower may bring welcome relief at one point and be ineffective at another point. The partner or father may be able to give her comfort that you can't. Don't let your feelings get hurt or let your ego get in the way. Your goal is to work with the laboring couple in any way that they need you, helping them have a positive birth.

As you gain experience, you will develop a pool of comforting techniques from which to draw, the most important one being to let the mother's body tell you what it needs.

Robin Elise Weiss, a doula who has attended more than 125 births, lists her top-ten doula tips for labor support:

10. Massage
9. Pelvic rocking
8. Double hip squeeze
7. Positioning
6. WATER!!
5. Frequent urination
4. Effleurage
3. Eating and drinking for comfort
2. Hot and/or cold packs/cloths

And the Number One doula tip is . . .

1. Support and encouragement

IT'S A BABY!

The birth is complete with the expulsion of the placenta. By then the baby has been out for some minutes. Encourage the parents to cuddle their newborn, and give them some space. You may have been asked to take some pictures; now is the best time. Congratulate them both, and let the mother talk about her experience. Most mothers are anxious to discuss, evaluate, and relive labor and delivery soon after the birth—if not immediately, within a few days. Encourage her to remember how well she did, how her body responded perfectly. Make the birth a mythic event with herself and her body as heroine. This is an event that she can look back on with pride.

The best time to start breastfeeding is in the first few moments after birth. It's a good way to comfort a newborn that may be unsettled from the birth. If the mother was medicated at all, the baby may not be very interested in nursing, but it's a good chance to practice breastfeeding positioning.

The mother may have short-lived physical reactions to the cessation of birth. Uncontrollable shaking is common. Don't let her become frightened. Shaking is okay and will go away soon. Call a nurse in to reassure her.

THE FOLLOW-UP VISIT

Your responsibilities also include giving the parents a written record of the birth. They will certainly treasure your account, and if questions ever arise about the circumstances surrounding the birth or the health of the baby, the report will be a vital part of your records and actions.

Most doulas call on the mother a couple of times during the first week at home with the baby. You are a valuable resource to her at that time because you can reassure her that she is doing everything right or you can help her with simple breastfeeding problems. If in the follow-up visits you feel she might need some additional support, you should have a list of available community resources. Breastfeeding consultants and mothers groups can make an immense difference in the new mother's adjustment to parenthood.

HELPING THE MOTHER ADJUST TO PARENTHOOD

Many doulas are tempted to act also as a couple's private childbirth educator and, later, as her lactation consultant and postpartum doula.

You may develop the knowledge and skills to fill all these roles; however, that is seldom in the mother's best interests. Particularly first-time mothers need to develop a support structure to help them with their adjustment to motherhood. If you allow yourself to become her sole resource, problems could develop when you aren't there or when your other clients need you. She needs many resources, and you can help her develop them. Encourage her to attend childbirth education classes. Not only is the breadth of knowledge gained well worth the time investment, but social time is built into these classes for parents to mingle and strike up friendships.

After birth, you help her get started with breastfeeding, but her ongoing questions and potential problems should be addressed by a lactation consultant. Mothering groups are often the basis for a new mom's support structure. Even second- and third-time mothers will join newborn mothering groups just for outside contact and reassurance. Helping the mother realize that she needs to purposely develop a social support group, that she can't depend solely on her pediatrician or on you, will help her adjust to her new role.

WHAT'S THE FIRST STEP?

Gather more information by contacting the groups and associations listed on page 87. DONA has a chat group online; so if you are hooked up to the Internet, you can speak directly to doulas about their experiences and thoughts. Most doulas start off by apprenticing and then going on for certification.

TRAINING AND CERTIFICATION

Several organizations certify doulas, but neither certification nor licensing is legally required. Many doulas-to-be simply apprentice themselves to experienced, established doulas.

Certification is usually a combination of study and hands-on experience. Certification varies with each group, but DONA's certification standards are typical:

1. Reading of four required books from DONA's list.
2. Completion of one of the following:

   Being certified in either childbirth education or midwifery
   Being a registered nurse with experience in labor and delivery
   Observing a recognized childbirth preparation course (not as a pregnant woman)
3. Attendance at a DONA-approved Labor Support training course of 14 or more hours that includes the following topics:

   The emotional and psychological process of labor and birth
   The anatomy and physiology of reproduction, labor, and birth
   Comfort measures and nonpharmacological pain-management techniques
   Appropriate topics for prenatal and postpartum discussion with clients
   Discussion of ethics and standards of practice for the doula
   Referral sources for client needs beyond the scope of the doula
   Communication skills and values clarification
4. Copies of good evaluations from (1) at least three clients to whom you've provided labor support, and (2) either three nurses and two physicians or three midwives (the evaluations to be completed after the training course).
5. Copies of documentation from three births at which you provided continuous labor support (the births having occurred after the training course).
6. A written essay (500 to 1,000 words) on the purpose and value of labor support.
7. Signature to the DONA Code of Ethics and Standards of Practice (their version of the medical doctor's Hippocratic oath).

Robin's Career

Doulas often come from related birth fields, and Robin Weiss is no exception. She first taught childbirth education (earning her ICCE) and then became a certified doula (DONA) nearly eight years ago. Along the way she has picked up her certification as a Bradley educator and as a childbirth assistant (NACA). She is finishing the work for a bachelor's degree in health education and is a doula trainer for DONA.

Robin became involved in the birthing field because she happened to witness a horrible birth: "I saw a birth by accident, someone I didn't even like, a neighbor. We were both in the Military Police Corps, and her husband was away in training. She had a four-day induction and during the four days would call me and ask me to bring her mail and sneak in food. I just happened to be there when she had the baby; they had given her some kind of narcotic and she was talking about stealing TVs in the red convertible. I just followed her into the delivery room. The certified nurse-midwife just sliced her open from stem to stern and delivered a tiny baby girl. The mother wasn't even aware of it. I never saw the mother again, but I knew that birth shouldn't be that way.

"I think of myself as a 'birth junkie.' I became a childbirth educator, then found out about birth doulas. I've just come from birth number 127 and it was a wonderful VBAC!"

Robin often needs to call on her charm and tact because nurses often think her efforts are crazy. She points out that you need to be patient and very nurturing to be a doula. Women who want to change the way things are tend to be drawn to becoming doulas.

In her area, births are very medicalized and women have

continued

few options. Robin notes, "Here, if you say you want a natural birth, all of your friends call you crazy! 'Just wait until the contractions start; then you'll change your mind.' 'Why be a martyr; epidurals don't hurt anybody!' But then a woman does it, and she is so thrilled in her new-found self. It gives everyone a new outlook, except for those friends who undermined her by saying 'Well, your labor was short; that's why you could do it' or 'You must have a really high pain threshold.'

"Empowerment is important. Despite what people believe, birth is more than bringing home a baby. Empowerment comes from being in control and a part of the decision-making process. It doesn't necessarily come from a vaginal birth; it comes from knowing that you made the right choices for you."

A doula's focus has to be on the mother, "I am there for YOU. If you need me for fetching, or massaging, hand holding, encouragement, information, I am there. I do not leave you, ever. I let YOU define my role."

Robin was the only doula in her area for a long time. Now there are several (she has trained many of them), but most couples want Robin because the others are still new. She has started the "double doula" theory in her area (she takes an apprentice doula with her). That way the new doulas get experience without being thrown into service unprepared. Because of the shortage of birth doulas, Robin hasn't had time to do a lot of postpartum doula work.

Because you can't schedule birth, the needs of her family sometimes conflict with the demands of her career. "My husband stays at home with the children, and I have devoted my entire career to doing this. It is difficult to leave on birthdays or when I want to go on vacation and ladies still haven't had their babies, but I am learning to deal with everything."

THE BUSINESS OF BEING A DOULA

If you decide to become a labor assistant or doula, along with the joy of attending births you will most likely have the satisfaction—and irritation—of running your own business. There are very few doula agencies, and only a few birth centers actually have doulas on staff. Doulas are usually independent.

Market Study

Before you become an independent doula, you will have to conduct a study of the doulas in your area:

How many doulas are in the area?
Are there enough births in your area to justify another doula?
Are doulas well-accepted in your area, or will you have to educate the public in order to build business?
What services are other doulas offering and for what fees?

Ask the local Chamber of Commerce for the number of births in your area; see if each local hospital is willing to tell you how many births they have per year. Discuss your intentions with the head labor-and-delivery nurse of each hospital. Find out from her how many other doulas practice in the area, what the hospital's attitude is toward doulas, how you can develop a good working relationship with the nurses, and what other staff members you should consult (and be friendly with).

You will probably find that the doulas in your area will be very helpful in getting you started. Nationally, there aren't nearly the number of doulas needed to fill the demand. Every doula needs a backup; linking up with one or more doulas to act first as their apprentice and then as their backup will get you started and give you insight into a successful doula practice.

Doulas generally offer the same services: one to two meetings before birth, labor assistance, and one follow-up visit. As an independent doula, you are free to offer more or fewer services, of course. In choosing among several doulas, the mother generally bases her decision on a good personality fit.

As you develop your business, you will need to discover what doctors, hospitals, birthing centers, and midwives are supportive of doulas and will consider referring business to you. Professional referrals are key to a continuing flow of clients. To encourage referrals, meet with doctors and midwives in your area, telling them about your training as a doula and what the scope of your services will be. Keep in mind that if they refer clients to you, you will be working with them and the mother. Be prepared to discuss how you plan to work with the doctor/midwife to benefit the mother and baby. Not all doctors/midwives welcome doulas. You may need to spend time and effort to educate these people, showing the studies that illustrate the benefits of involvement of doulas in birth.

Marketing

Marketing encompasses every aspect of your business that a client can see. It includes everything from telephone listings to talk-show appearances. Marketing is the face you put on for the world. Make sure you are professional, well-trained, and competent. Appearing warm and friendly is an important aspect of your business profile, too, so don't get too carried away and present yourself as if you were from the corporate world!

Here is a list of marketing ideas to get you started. The best ideas are often stolen from completely different fields (cookie stores pump the scent of baking cookies out their front door, just as perfume samplers in department store aisles spray you with the latest scent). So pay attention to marketing in the world around you and be creative:

- Have business cards made up. Have letterhead stationery printed for follow-up letters to health care professionals. Call Paper Direct at 1-900-A-PAPERS for their catalog of preprinted paper so you can make professional looking brochures and business cards on your desktop computer.
- Print your birth report for the parents on nice-looking letterhead. This makes it appropriate for the baby memory book and ensures that other parents will see and admire it. During your client interviews, show how attractive it will look; it is part of your package.
- Make up flyers and brochures to leave with childbirth educators, with doctors and midwives, and with lactation consultants.
- Attend any local baby fairs with your flyers. Join up with a diaper service or other local company to share booth space.
- Advertise in the Yellow Pages, in appropriate local parenting newsletters, and in newspapers.
- Offer to speak at childbirth education classes.
- Call the local newspaper and radio/television talk shows, and offer yourself as an expert. You'd be surprised at how interested they will be—don't forget, they have to fill hours of programming day after day.
- Hold your own birth seminars with you as the featured speaker. Include related professionals, like childbirth educators and lactation consultants.

WHERE DO I WORK?

As a doula, you only need a home office with an answering machine. When you meet with your clients before birth for either interviews or preparatory sessions, you can meet at their home. Of course, during labor and delivery, you will meet the laboring woman first in her home and go with her to the hospital or to her chosen place of birth.

HOW MUCH DO I CHARGE?

Doulas may charge a flat fee or an hourly rate. Many prefer a flat fee so the mother isn't punished for a long labor. In 1996, nationally the fee ranged from $200 to $800. An hourly rate would be between $15 and $30 per hour, with a minimum amount of hours (usually 20 or more), depending on the geographic location. Some doulas choose to barter, others have developed a sliding scale based on ability to pay. You may be able to develop a relationship with several obstetricians who believe in the benefits of doulas and will write a prescription for your services. In those cases, health insurance may cover your services.

You should require a deposit when the client reserves your time. With the deposit in hand, you block out a two- to four-week period during which the client's labor is likely to start; you must then turn away other potential clients due during the same time period. You bill for the balance of the fee after the birth. In rare occurrences, it may be necessary to return the deposit, but only if you were called for labor and were unavailable (illness, car trouble). Otherwise, your time has been hired, so you charge your fee no matter the outcome of the birth (if, perhaps, it didn't meet all of the mother's expectations) even if you missed the birth because the parents had no time to call you or because they forgot. On the rare occasion where a baby dies, some doulas suggest donating the fee to a charity of the parent's choice. Certainly that is a personal decision.

RESOURCES

ASSOCIATIONS AND ORGANIZATIONS FOR DOULAS

Association of Childbirth Companions
44 Maple Street
Whitefield, NH 03598
603-837-9511

Birth Support Providers International
3941 Park Drive #20-114
El Dorado Hills, CA 95762
916-974-8143

Certified Perinatal Educators Association
3941 Park Drive #20-114
El Dorado Hills, CA 95762
916-974-8143

Doulas of North America
1100 23rd Avenue East
Seattle, WA 98112
206-324-5440

Informed Home Birth/Informed Birth and Parenting
P.O. Box 3675
Ann Arbor, MI 48106
313-662-6857

National Association of Childbirth Assistants
P.O. Box 1537
Boyes Hot Springs, CA 95416
707-939-0543

Seattle Midwifery School
2524 16th Avenue S.
Suite 300
Seattle, WA 98144
206-322-8834

BOOKS

Becoming a Childbirth Assistant by C. M. Lowe. Mail check or money order for $24.95 and $3.50 postage and handling to: C. M. Lowe, 3941 Park Drive #20-114, El Dorado Hills, CA 95762.

5

HELPING THE NEW FAMILY FORM: THE HOME DOULA

What will you do?	Assist the new mom at home
How many hours a week?	Variable, from part- to full-time
Your work hours?	Traditional
Will you need licensing/ certification?	None required
What can you earn?	$10–$15 per hour
Liability insurance needed?	No personal insurance required

MOTHERING THE MOTHER

Home doulas mother the new mother. During the baby's first few weeks at home, the home doula, or postpartum doula, is there to advise the new mom on baby care and to be the oil that keeps the family running. Doulas fill a traditional healing role that extended families or close communities historically provided. The mother and father remain the primary caretakers of the new baby, and the home doula relieves the new mother of all other at-home burdens so that she can concentrate on her newborn.

If you decide to become a home doula, you will be expected to know what the new mother needs before she knows it. In all of the careers working in the birth field, this one calls for the greatest variety of skills. You are teacher, protector, keeper of the home. You will be called on to troubleshoot with breastfeeding and to wash dishes. It is not a glamorous job, but it offers constant exposure to mother and child in those first tender weeks. Most doulas are "baby junkies" who value the bringing of a child into a family as a ritual and a privilege to watch and support.

Following birth, mothers need to be nurtured and cared for so that they can turn that warmth to the new child. The more the mother is cared for, the more easily she can manage the baby. In the book *Mothering the Mother* by Klaus, Kennell, and Klaus, research was reported on women's feelings leaving the hospital with a newborn. Almost every mother agreed with the statement "I have not had time to get to know my baby and to know what to do with my baby at home." Consider the implications of that statement in the context of a woman who is expected to resume running the household after grueling hours (perhaps days) of labor. Remember also that family and friends will feel duty-bound to visit the newborn; so the mother—physically exhausted, uncertain of how to care for the infant, overwhelmed with emotional responses to hormonal changes—feels she is expected to serve cookies and entertain!

In traditional cultures (as it was in American culture up until the

1920s), new mothers are accorded a lying-in period. During this time, the other women in the family move in to help with the running of the household and the taking care of the baby. These women with experience would be constantly available to validate the new mother's emotions and to assure her that her extreme feelings are normal. They would be there as a listener so the mother can have the pleasure of reliving the birth and each of the firsts: first feed, first bath and so on. From their experience they could help her with breastfeeding and other baby-care issues. With their shared labor, the household work would be done. Most cultures have slowly moved away from these family traditions.

In America several cultural trends, starting in the 1920s and gaining momentum through the 1950s, tore these traditions apart: society changed from an agricultural one, with interdependent communities, to one of business and manufacturing—the isolation of city and suburban life made asking for help a weakness instead of a right. The moving of births from home to hospital made birthing an assembly-line process (labor in one room, down the hall to the delivery room, down the hall to the recovery room, down to the maternity floor for postpartum), dehumanizing birth and taking birth out of the community. Commonly available transportation moved families farther apart. Women working outside of the home didn't have the flexibility to assist a sister or a friend. Women began having babies at older ages, so new grandmothers were likely to be older (more years separating her from her birth experiences), and her time was likely to be taken up by a job outside the home so she was only available for a few days of help, if at all.

Though the traditional support systems for new mothers have largely disappeared, the need for such support still exists. Enter the professional home doula: a woman trained and experienced in the postpartum needs of women and babies. Because the doula is paid, there is no question of the new mother feeling that she must be the hostess to a helping family member. Both the mother and the doula can concentrate on the well-being of the mother and the baby. The first doulas were simply women who loved newborns and helping a new family bond. Training, still not required, became more available along with certification in the 1980s.

Doula agencies began appearing in the early 1980s in New York and Boston. Most large cities have several doula agencies and many practicing independent doulas. In some parts of the country, doula services are still just developing.

WHAT YOU DO AS A HOME–HEALTH CARE DOULA

As the doula you are a caregiver, whatever that entails. Your responsibility is to assess what the mother needs to relieve her of stress and to help her heal. A study by Johnson & Johnson revealed that about 80 percent of the participating women reported either psychological or lifestyle concerns at either two or eight weeks after birth. Most women complained that they felt limited in the activities they could perform; they were reluctant to entertain visitors; and they felt tied to the house. As many as 16 percent were depressed or concerned about depression at two weeks. Further concerns focused on their limited ability to interact with their older children and their husband. Not surprisingly, concerns were raised about their body image—about being damaged or out of shape. Child care was also becoming an issue.

Ideally, the doula determines what needs to be done without being told. After completing labor and delivery, a mother is physically and emotionally drained. Having to give orders and organize the household, even with a doula performing the work, adds pressure to the new mother. She needs to be nurtured and protected just as she needs to nurture and protect her child. Your support falls into three categories of care: physical, emotional, and social.

Physical

Extreme fatigue is normal for a new mother. Rest and sleep are both physically and emotionally restorative. There are many simple steps a new mom can take to ensure her continuing healing. You need to remind her to take care of herself because her primary attention will probably focus on the baby. Some of the subjects with which you will need to be familiar in order to help the new mother are: perineal self-care, lochial flow, breast changes, diet, rest, elimination, and medication.

You'll need to monitor the mother during this postpartum period (up to eight weeks after delivery). Many of the common postpartum complaints can be avoided if the mother takes the correct preventative steps or is alert for early signs of problems. For example, constipation is extremely common because of the mother's decreased muscle tone, dehydration, and the possible effects of medication and anesthesia. You can help ward off constipation, and the hemorrhoids it often leads to, by urging the mother to drink six to eight glasses of fluids a day, to walk, and to perform leg and abdominal exercises. Few mothers will have the motivation and awareness level to take these sensible precautions without gentle reminders. Other minor complaints that can possibly be alleviated before they turn into big problems are: episiotomy care, engorgement, mastitis, and urinary tract infection.

A first-time mother will call upon you to teach her many of the basics of baby care: nail clipping, umbilical cord care, bathing, and so on. Don't be surprised or frustrated if a new mother asks questions that you know were answered in the hospital or in the day or two following birth. For a variety of physical and emotional reasons, very little of what a new mom is told during the first couple of days postpartum will stay with her. You will undermine her confidence if you point out that she already was told this. When teaching baby care, it is important not to take over, but to let the mother do the handling of the baby. Being nonintrusive and nonjudgmental will help her learn to trust herself.

Don't forget to include the dad or partner in the baby-care lessons. Learning from an outsider like you eliminates any possible power struggle between the parents. Although his help may not be strictly necessary now because you are there to help, getting him involved from the start initiates a healthy pattern of mutual support and care for the baby.

More experienced mothers are likely to be more confident with their baby. They will enjoy remembering how tiny a newborn is and how new everything is for the baby. These moms will be more comfortable letting you take care of the house and older children while she gets to know her new baby.

For those moms who are breastfeeding, it's "lots and lots of breastfeeding support," notes Lisa Fearon, a doula in Westchester County, New York. Helping moms get off to a good start with breastfeeding will forestall problems that could occur down the road. If you don't have personal experience with breastfeeding, and even if you do, it's best to become certified as a lactation consultant. You will also want to develop a network of experts to call upon when asked a question you don't know how to answer.

All mothers need nutritional meals and lots of fluids if they are breastfeeding. It's easy for mothers to forget to take care of themselves with the demands of a new baby. It may seem like too much work for her to make a meal for herself. You can make sure she is meeting her own nutritional requirements. You may need to go to the supermarket for her and to plan and cook meals. Cook extra so that there are leftovers to have for lunch the next day or to freeze for future meals. While she is breastfeeding, have liquids—water, broth, juice—ready for her, and offer them without being asked. Your foresight will be appreciated.

You may also be called upon to chauffeur mother and baby to their various doctor appointments. If the mother has had a cesarean section, she won't be allowed to drive for a period of time. She will still need to take the baby for a well-baby checkup and to see her own obstetrician for follow-up.

All other aspects of housekeeping, such as light cleaning and laundry, will fall to you also. The baby will generate lots of laundry. In addition, new baby clothing brought as gifts need to be laundered in baby soap before being worn.

Emotional

Most mothers need to talk about the birth, to reexperience it. Birth is the most formidable physical challenge most women will ever face. The physical and emotional aftermath of delivery leaves many women with the type of high experienced by Olympic-level athletes. The high fades in a few hours, but it leaves some women with feelings of empowerment and strength that, with positive reinforcement, can last for a lifetime.

Having a baby is one of the greatest joys parents will experience. Mothers and fathers need to share their joy by talking about it. Many doulas think that this is the most important aspect of their job. With family members far flung and friends at their own jobs, new parents need someone outside their own family unit to tell about the labor and delivery.

Following birth, most mothers will undergo extreme mood swings. Usually these are blamed on hormonal changes caused by the body adjusting to not being pregnant any longer. Certainly some mood-shift blame should be placed on the realization (both fearful and joyful) that she has a baby (or another baby) to care for. Whatever the cause, you need to reassure her that these swings are normal and that she will get past them. Reassure the father, too, that it is unlikely that he or his actions are causing the swings.

Help her create a private space, a corner in her bedroom or a comfortable spot in a not-often-used living room, where she can retreat by herself or with the baby to be alone. Allow her that time to retreat, and protect her by keeping others away when she is there.

Watch the mother for signs of blues that last too long, or that descend several weeks after labor. Your appropriate intervention could head off long-term mental problems triggered by the birth.

Social

Visitors can be a blessing and a curse. Offer to monitor and shield the new mom from visitors when she and the baby are resting. Encourage her to limit visiting hours even at home so that she can get the rest she needs during the first couple of weeks. You can also suggest that she stay in her nightgown and robe for several days so any visitors realize that she is a person who needs rest. Soon, she'll be anxious to get dressed up and to see all of her friends and family.

New mothers need a lot of support. Suggesting groups to join and helping the mother to develop her own support network (comprised of family, doctors, experts, and neighborhood mothers) will keep her from becoming isolated. Regular contact with other mothers will help her get answers and perspectives that just one person (you) can't offer. Remember, you will probably only be with her a few weeks. You must prepare her for a lifetime.

Even experienced mothers have to be reminded that they still need a support network. They will have forgotten how demanding a newborn can be. And their older child or children will create a new set of concerns. Anticipate that the older child will regress, forgetting some skills that were firmly established, and encourage the parents to be positive and patient. These moms may need you to take over primary care for the newborn while they give the older child much-needed attention. Take your cue from the mothers.

Birth and breastfeeding are viewed differently in different cultures. It is likely that at some point you will have a client who comes from a culture with which you aren't completely familiar: People cope with pain in silence in some cultures and with loud noises in others. Some cultures throw away the early breast milk (colostrum) until the transitional milk comes in; other cultures bury the placenta in the backyard. On the other hand, it is potentially insulting to assume a woman with a particular cultural background will act in a stereotypical way. When unsure, be slow to judge, and simply ask the mother what she prefers.

Lisa's Career

Lisa Fearon is the founder and owner of The Tenth Month, Inc., a postpartum-care agency. She is a doula herself and has twelve employee doulas. Lisa believes that doulas are "the up-and-coming need.

"I first read about postpartum doulas four years ago. I was pregnant for the first time and did a lot of reading about pregnancy and birth. I lost the baby, and that led me to reevaluate my life and my priorities. It was an epiphany! At the time I had a high-stress job, and I felt that had a lot to do with losing the baby. I decided I wanted to take the stress out of my life, find a business I could run from home, so when I got pregnant again I would be able to stay home with the baby.

"I remembered how much I had enjoyed teaching nursery school early in my career. Because of that, my interest with getting pregnant again, and my love of babies, being a doula fit right in. At first I was both a labor doula and a postpartum doula."

Lisa does not work as a labor doula anymore. "It is physically too difficult. After labor, I'm nearly as tired as the mother! When she is sent home from the hospital twenty-four hours later, I'm still recovering. I can't give her all the care she needs. You need to be fresh and energetic for new moms. You have many tasks to complete for her in a short window of time.

"Now I refer birth doula inquiries to a competent specialist and focus on postpartum doula work. It wasn't difficult to choose which doula to be. I'm like most doulas—I love all the babies, we all love the babies!"

Lisa has trained with the National Association of Postpartum Care Services (NAPCS) and worked through their certification program. "I've done an extensive training with the National Association of Childbirth Assistants (NACA). I am a member of DONA and have read everything I can get my hands on about postpartum. I've also attended several seminars on breastfeeding with our local breastfeeding consortium and attended several conferences on birth and postpartum. One such conference was in Seattle, Washington; it was jointly sponsored by NAPCS, DONA, and PALS (Pacific Alliance of Labor Support).

"I work as a doula about twenty hours a week. That's four hours a day, five days a week. It's a physically demanding job. I might typically have several clients at a time, but I don't like to take on too many. If I'm not there enough, it is difficult for the mom to get comfortable with me or for me to know her preferences."

Lisa finds the job calls on a variety of skills. "We do a lot of laundry! Light housekeeping is a big part of the job. And so much of what we do is breastfeeding support. Most often, moms do the infant care. My focus is on making sure she is eating right, a lot of nutrition education, breastfeeding support, making meals, housekeeping. I make sure the mom does a lot of the infant care and that she is comfortable doing it. I drive the mom to appointments with the pediatrician and with the obstetrician. My focus is to facilitate a lot of rest and recuperation for the mother. A doula lets the mom focus on the baby. I spend a lot of time coaxing the mother back into bed. I know I'm doing my job when the mom falls asleep when I'm there. If she's asleep, she trusts you.

"A good doula doesn't need to be managed. She is intuitive and knows what the mother needs before she needs it.

"It's different for first-time mothers versus second-timers: first-timers need more education and breastfeeding support. I teach basics of infant care, including the first bath, the clipping of the nails, and umbilical cord care.

continued

"Second-time moms generally need much less education and training. They still need a lot of emotional support. Generally, this mom needs the doula to focus on the older child and keep the rhythm of things balanced. Lots of moms just sit and hold the baby for the first few weeks. A doula lets her do that—when she's ready to have me hold the baby, she'll tell me.

"A doula takes the cues from mom whether she needs emotional support or work around the house. I always make sure that I interface with the dads too; they appreciate the training.

"I always planned to turn my business into an agency, and after a short time of being a doula on my own, I started the Tenth Month. There is plenty of business in my area, but my focus has been more on the quality of help we provide versus crash staffing to meet the quantity of requests. We have a staff of twelve. I have very high training standards for my doulas. Of course they have to be certified. I also have speakers come in for continuing education. This month we have an herbal therapist coming in. Next month we've scheduled a psychotherapist to discuss family issues from pets on up."

Lisa is a new mom herself. "Yes, I've given birth to an eight-pound, ten-ounce baby girl, Caleigh Olivia, who is ten months old. We had a labor support doula assist in the birth and I was able to have a fully natural, unmedicated birth. I am still breastfeeding Caleigh and our postpartum doula got both of us off to a great start."

HOW DO I FIND CLIENTS?

If you choose to work for an agency (in most parts of the country that won't be an option because they don't even exist yet), you won't need to find your own clients—the agency should handle all the marketing for you. However, most home doulas work independently or in loose groups and need to market to find their own clients.

Speak with other home doulas who are already established. They may have too many clients and be able to refer potential clients to you. Be prepared to work with an established doula for a reduced fee or even as an apprentice for free to prove your skills and to earn the established doula's confidence before she will refer clients.

Make up business cards and brochures (call Paper Direct at 1-900-A-PAPERS for their catalog of preprinted paper so you can make professional-looking brochures and business cards on your desktop computer).

Offer to speak about parenting skills at childbirth education classes. Take your brochures and business cards to distribute and to leave behind for other classes.

Attend local baby fairs with your flyers. Join up with a diaper service or other local company to share booth space.

Ask satisfied clients to refer you to their pregnant friends, and ask for letters of reference to show in client interviews.

Ideally, the mother will interview and select her home doula before the birth of the baby. Expect her to interview several doulas. The mother will likely be seeking a doula who can be supportive but not overbearing; one who will fit in well with her family and who has experience in the areas she may be most concerned about; one whom she can trust with her child and in whom she can confide her concerns and thoughts.

During an interview, be prepared to answer such questions as:

How often have you served as a home doula before?
What, exactly, do your services cover?
Do you have transportation for yourself?
Do you have transportation to take the mother and the baby to their respective doctor appointments?
Can you cook meals?

Can you help the mother breastfeed?
Are you skilled at new-baby care?
Can you spot possible health problems, such as jaundice?
How much direction do you need?
Are you certified in infant CPR/first aid?
Have you an up-to-date tuberculosis test?
Do you have a police record?
Do you offer additional services, such as infant or maternal massage, or aromatherapy? Do you charge extra for massage, etc.?
(If there are other children) What is your experience with caring for older children?

Have ready a list of three to five referrals from satisfied clients and/or health professionals. Be prepared with your own questions for the mother and her family. You will want to ascertain if your parenting style will mesh with hers, if her expectations for your support are realistic, if you will like working with this woman and her family. With experience, you will be able to tell before working with the family if your skills match their needs. You will be intimately involved with the family for several weeks. If you anticipate a clash in parenting styles or unrealistic expectations, you may decide it's better to refer the family to another doula.

SHOULD I WORK INDEPENDENTLY OR WITH AN AGENCY?

Doulas may work independently or for a doula agency. There are many advantages of working for an agency, particularly if you are just starting out. The agency takes care of advertising and promotion, thus assuring you of a steady stream of work. Most agencies offer continuing education through guest lecturers or seminars. You would work within a community of doulas so you can share your experiences and get ideas from like-minded women. You have access to more experienced doulas who can help you with questions to which you may not know the answer. Because of the growing demand for doulas, work may be readily available. Often, women who run doula agencies complain that they need to recruit doulas constantly to keep up with the demand.

Working for an agency may not be an option in many parts of the country unless you form your own doula agency. If you do, try to link up with a hospital or a birth center to have them include your services as part of a package of services. Get the hospital to go to bat for you with insurance companies.

Whether working for an agency or independently, before starting to work as a doula, you will want to be certified and/or competent in breastfeeding support, infant CPR, and first aid; to have a valid driver's license and possibly access to a car; and to be capable of housecleaning and cooking simple meals.

TRAINING AND CERTIFICATION

One of the few organizations that certify home doulas is the National Association of Postnatal Care Services (NAPCS). In order to become certified by NAPCS, you must first become a member and fill out a Certification Packet ($10 fee for the packet). Upon completing the application and other forms in the Certification Packet, the caregiver must take and pass a written exam and an oral interview ($40 fee for the exam). The primary areas assessed in the exams are: physical health of the new mother; postpartum family dynamics and emotions; infant care and behavior; and infant feeding. Several seminars are available to assist your study. Most women take six months or so to complete their readings and pass the exam. Once the exam is passed, the certification is valid for three years.

If you are considering starting your own doula service, NAPCS offers a Service Accreditation. It is designed to ensure that a competency level for ethical business practices is established. Issues addressed include: consumer rights, quality assurance, minimal competency, and continuing education of staff. The Service Accreditation Packet outlines the criteria, tools, and fees required. Packets are available to NAPCS members for a $5 fee (applied toward the $75 application fee) and must be requested through the Accreditation Chair. Upon approval and receipt of a $150 fee for the three-year term, a certificate will be forwarded.

HOW MUCH DO I CHARGE?

Most home doulas work for an hourly wage of between $10 to $15. Usually a doula sets a minimum number of hours, generally four-hour shifts with a two-week minimum. It is best not to let it drop below that, or you will spend your time servicing too many clients and not getting to know them well enough to do the best job for them. You may need to adjust your hourly and minimum rate (up or down) to reflect the realities of your community.

If you offer additional services, such as infant or mother massage or aromatherapy, you can charge an additional fee. You may want to compare fees with other professionals to keep your fees in line with others in the community.

Encourage your clients to file a request for reimbursement of home doula fees with their insurance company. Many insurance companies consider doulas as homemakers and, therefore, do not cover their services. However, filing requests for reimbursement will create a trail and will build awareness of home doulas at insurance companies. The quantity of requests for reimbursement could lead insurance companies to realize how many parents use doulas and to study the positive effect doulas have in lowering postpartum follow-up costs.

INTRODUCING PETS TO BABY

Pets are members of the family who will be affected by the birth of the baby. Many pets are lavished with attention and care before the birth of the first baby. After the birth, they will lose their position as "baby" in the family, and some effort should be made to prepare the pet for the change. An older pet will almost never hurt a harmless baby. A well-tempered dog that doesn't tend to snap, or a cat that doesn't scratch, should be fine with a baby. Any direct threat to a child might more likely come from an older sibling or cousin teasing or startling the pet. Watch for signs that an older sibling, even though well trained not to harass a dog or cat, might be regressing or taking out aggravation on the pet.

Cats are usually not interested in babies—forget the old wives' tale about cats sleeping with babies and smothering them. They are likely to keep their distance.

In preparation for a first baby, have the parents start before the birth by training the pet to stay out of the baby's room. Keeping the pet out of the room will limit the baby's exposure to pet hair (potentially allergy-triggering) and will ease the mother's concern about the pet examining the infant unsupervised or even jumping into the crib. Waiting until the baby is born and then trying to keep a pet out of the room will only cause the pet to become jealous. You may want to suggest a screen door on the baby's room so Mom can see in and pets are kept out.

Before the baby comes home from the hospital, take the baby's blanket home and let the dog and/or the cat sniff it to get used to the scent. When parents take the baby home for the first time, counsel them to use the same common sense they would if there were an older child. Mom's arms should be free to hug and greet the pet. She should spend the first few minutes giving the pet attention. The baby should be presented to the pet for an introductory sniff (under close supervision). Expect the pet to display some anxiety immediately and for the next few days. Having some treats on hand for the pet may reassure it.

Don't forget that your presence in the home will be confusing and potentially threatening to a pet also (dogs might become aggressive; cats might just hide). It is worth a preparatory trip just before the birth of the baby so that your scent is fresh in the pet's memory.

It's best if you can time your pet visit to coincide with the pet's dinner time. If you feed it dinner, you have gone a long way toward making a friend.

All pets should have had a recent checkup with the veterinarian and should be up-to-date on all its shots. However, the risk of a pet exposing the baby to a disease is low. There are no documented records of a pet passing either Lyme disease, feline leukemia, or feline AIDS to a human. If a pet has not been wormed, there is a risk to the infant if the child touches the pet's stools and then puts his hand in his mouth. Have the mother check with her vet.

Other than these hints, just counsel the parents to use common sense: to spend time with the pet and treat it like the cherished older child it is for many people.

RESOURCES

Doulas of North America (DONA)
1100 23rd Avenue East
Seattle, WA 98112
206-324-5440
World Wide Web site: http://www.dona.com

National Association for Postpartum Services
P.O. Box 1012
Edmonds, WA 98020
800-45-DOULA

6

HELPING PARENTS WITH THE HARDEST JOB IN THE WORLD: PARENT AND FAMILY LIFE EDUCATOR

What will you do?	Teach parenting skills through classes and home visits
How many hours a week?	10–20 hours
Your work hours?	Variable; may be evenings and weekends
Will you need licensing/ certification?	May be required in some school districts; advisable in any case; most parent educators have a degree in education or counseling
Wha[illegible]n you earn?	$10–$15 per hour
Liability insurance needed?	No personal insurance required

Conception is but a moment in our lives. Childbirth takes only a few hours, if we're lucky. But parenting? Well, that's forever. And it's the hardest job any of us will ever have.

Even in the best-case scenario—a stable couple with sufficient resources—parents face a monumental task in raising a child. Fortunately, parents who seek guidance may find help through local parent education programs.

Some form of parent education is probably already available in your community. If you're a new parent, chances are you know of some parenting classes, either through your pediatrician, childbirth educator, local school district, or community center. If you're an educator—a schoolteacher, a childbirth instructor, or a day-care staffer—perhaps you've offered classes in parenting. If parent education is not available in your community, it's a field ripe for development. And it's a great new opportunity, offering flexible scheduling and hours to suit the needs of a former teacher or counselor or otherwise formerly employed person inching back into the workforce.

WHY THE NEED?

The world has always been a hard place for children; it has become an even harder place these days, with greater expectations for achievement. Time was when a child started kindergarten and first grade and learned to read. Now, in many communities, children are expected to know how to read by the time they reach first grade. And they had better know how to play well with their classmates, too. These high expectations—created both by parents and by society at large—have compelled communities and school districts around the country to establish early intervention programs designed to help parents prepare their children for what lies ahead.

That's why there's been a spate of new offerings from community centers, schools and school districts, and health centers for striving parents. First, we'll review some national programs that present career opportunities in parent education. Then, for those who are already experienced educators, we'll give some ideas for new program offerings that can be made available through local community centers, Ys, churches, medical centers, and schools.

PARENTS AS TEACHERS

Parents As Teachers (PAT), a voluntary, early childhood, parent education program, has received widespread attention in the past few years—and has achieved results so impressive that President Bill Clinton has provided funds for it in his ambitious Goal 2000, a bill that legislates for major education reform in the United States. PAT has a national base to support local communities in developing their own parent education programs.

The guiding philosophy of PAT is that parents are their children's first and most influential teachers. Recognizing that teaching does not come naturally to all parents, PAT believes that teaching, to be effective, should be a partnership of the home, the school, and the community. And this partnership should start early. Educational research has revealed:

- By age three, a child will have absorbed and recognized about 1,000 spoken words—two-thirds of the adult everyday speaking vocabulary.
- By age four, a child's brain will have grown to nearly three-fourths of its adult size.
- If a child suffers an undetected developmental delay, such as a delay in language development or problem-solving skills, overcoming these problems at school entry is much more difficult than through intervention at an earlier stage.

In Missouri, where the PAT program started, that last point made a real impact: a relatively small amount of money invested relatively early, the research showed, might be able to save school districts much more in special education programs later on. The typical cost for one year for the PAT program is $190 per family. The cost of special education can run into the thousands.

Results of Missouri's PAT program have been impressive. A 1985 study showed that children participating in the PAT program scored significantly higher at age three than a comparison group on all measures of intelligence, achievement, language ability, and positive social development. A 1989 follow-up study showed that first graders who had been in the PAT program scored significantly higher on standardized measures of reading and math achievement. Further, PAT parents were more likely to request parent-teacher conferences and to be involved in school activities.

Now, PAT programs are mandated statewide in Missouri; school districts must provide them. While family participation is voluntary, 40 percent of families with children do participate.

In 1987, PAT went national. It is now available in communities in forty-five states and five other countries.

Through the partnership of home, school, and community, PAT strives to empower parents to give their child the best possible start in life. PAT advocates believe that, in so doing, parents are laying the foundation for a child's success in school and in life. PAT improves parents' knowledge of child development and appropriate ways to stimulate learning, promotes a strong parent-child relationship, increases parents' confidence, develops a partnership between parents and school, and provides a means for early detection of potential learning problems.

The PAT Program

The PAT program has four components: home visits, group meetings, developmental screenings, and a resource network.

Home visits

PAT-trained parent educators visit each assigned family's home on a regular basis. By far the most popular aspect of PAT, the home visit allows the parent educator to individualize and personalize the program for each family and child. It provides the opportunity to support parents as they take the child development and child-rearing information specific to their own child and use it within their own family. Parents better understand what can be expected from a child at each stage of development. Appropriate parent-child learning activities are also a part of the visit.

The number and frequency of visits—weekly, biweekly, or monthly—depend on the needs and desires of the family, as well as on the funding for the program in that particular community. Some families prefer that visits not take place in the home; arrangements can be made to have them in a local church, school, or community center. Once mutual trust has been established, the visits usually move to the home.

Group meetings

Group meetings for parents are designed to allow families to share successes and common concerns about their children's behavior and development and to provide a means for additional input from staff and from outside speakers. Parent-child activities may be a part of these group meetings. These activities reinforce the importance of family interaction. Group meetings can also be designed specifically for dads or for moms separately. Some PAT group meetings have "drop in and play" components, which provide parents the opportunity to talk with other parents and with educators, knowing that the children are nearby and cared for. This can be an important outlet for families.

Developmental screenings

Developmental screenings serve two purposes: to reassure parents that the child is developing on target and to identify problems early enough to assist parents with appropriate interventions. Developmental screening is performed every year beginning at age one. Parents are encouraged to observe and monitor the child's development on an ongoing basis. Parent and parent-educator observations during the first years of life, coupled with periodic screening, serve to ensure against undetected delays or learning difficulties that may interfere with success in school.

Resource network

In serving families, PAT programs help parents link with other community resources that provide services beyond the scope of PAT. These include speech and hearing clinics, diagnostic services, programs for children with special needs, lending libraries and learning resources for children and parents, health and mental health agencies, social service agencies, and so on.

How to Become a PAT Educator

To participate as a parent educator in the PAT program, you must be certified through PAT. Several training programs are available:

"Parents As Teachers Institute: Birth to Three" teaches about early childhood development (birth to age three), processes of effective home visits, literacy-building activities, facilitation of parent-child interactions, ideas for parent group meetings, effective use of community resources, and evaluation of program effectiveness. After successfully completing the program, you will receive renewable one-year certification as a PAT parent educator. This certification program requires thirty-one hours of instruction over five days. The cost is $425.

"Parents As Teachers Institute: Three to Five" extends the PAT program upward to kindergarten and is available only to persons certified as parent educators birth to age three. Training in child development appropriate to this age group is added, as are opportunities to experience how children learn, techniques for facilitating parent-child interaction during home visits, and ways to promote literacy. The cost of the training program, which involves fifteen hours of training over two days, is $200 and includes all materials.

"Parents As Teachers for Adolescent Parents" is for professionals who will implement PAT programs and deliver services to adolescent parents with children from birth to age three.

There is also a program designed for non-PAT professionals working with families in the home, including those involved in programs such as Head Start or Even Start. This program, "Instructional Home Visiting and Effective Parent Involvement," provides techniques for helping parents be effective teachers of their children, guidelines for conducting personal visits in the home, problem solving with parents, and observation of videotaped home visits by experienced parent education. This two-day training program may cost about $200.

Finally, "Birth to Three" and "Three to Five" institutes are available for those involved in Even Start, other Title I programs, or Head Start. Depending on the financial resources available in the local PAT program, fees for these courses are usually covered by the local school district.

Who Can Become a PAT Parent Educator?

Patricia Holman, of PAT's public education office, says that the most successful parent educators usually have college degrees (though that is not a requirement). Those with experience working with parents and their children from birth to age five in a supervised setting also do well. This may be as a school teacher, a counselor, or a social worker. Keep in mind that requirements for local programs vary. In Texas, PAT educators must be school teachers or social workers. If a PAT program is in place in your community, it may have well-defined guidelines in place.

Will You Make a Good Parent Educator?

The PAT program suggests the following as characteristics of successful parent educators:

- Communications skills
  - Is active listener
  - Is empathetic
  - Establishes rapport
  - Builds relationships
  - Asks open-ended questions
  - Provides information regarding child development and appropriate child-rearing practices
  - Individualizes presentation of information so it will be appropriate for each family
  - Tolerates silences
- Observational skills
  - Observes strengths of parent and child
  - Recognizes behavior or development of child differing from the expected norm
  - Identifies inappropriate parental expectations
  - Is sensitive to family's cultural patterns and unique family needs
- Interpersonal skills
  - Is enthusiastic
  - Is confident in ability to serve families
  - Is nonjudgmental, compassionate, and respectful
  - Maintains sense of humor
  - Maintains appropriate boundaries

continued

- Empowerment of parents

  Enables parents to be astute observers of their own child

  Promotes parents' confidence to make informed decisions

  Encourages parents to be involved in activities with their child

  Helps parents to network with other parents

  Helps parents use community resources

- Knowledge of:

  Child development, appropriate childrearing practices, and issues

  Community resources

  Appropriate use of screening materials

- Professionalism

  Maintains realistic expectations for self and families being served

  Practices confidentiality

  Manages stress

  Plans and implements services according to program guidelines

  Promotes the parenting program

  Actively shares skills, knowledge, and resources with colleagues

  Maintains well-organized and comprehensive records

  Reads and attends workshops, seminars, and so on, to enhance own understanding of child development and child-rearing issues and practices

  Takes initiative to research materials and community resources needed to address parental needs, concerns, and questions

ACTIVE PARENTING—A VIDEO-BASED PROGRAM

If your school district does not have a program such as PAT and, for economic or other reasons, is not likely to for a while, hospitals, churches, or other community organizations may be using parent education programs such as Active Parenting. This video-based program provides a somewhat less comprehensive, but still worthwhile, means of guiding parents. The goal is to help parents and educators with the "most important job of their lives—raising and educating children." The goal of parent education, according to Active Parenting, is to raise children who are "courageous, responsible, and cooperative within relationships that are based on mutual respect."

The Active Parenting programs use video/discussion as a teaching medium. The video program presents scenarios and cues the parent educator to turn the tape off for discussion in the classroom. Obviously a less comprehensive program than PAT—and one that does not provide the one-on-one attention provided by a program like PAT—this program is still a good entree for communities seeking to develop some kind of parent education program.

The foundation of this video-based program is the Active Parenting Today program kit, a video-based parent education program that has reached more than a million parents around the world. As with PAT, the basic materials are used to develop local programs that answer the needs of the community. The program kit includes two videos, a leader's guide, a parent's guide (recommended for each parent participating in the program), a drug-prevention booklet, completion certificates for parents, and promotional and publicity materials.

In addition to providing the video materials for parents, educators, and community leaders, Active Parenting provides leadership-training workshops and support for the video-based programs. These workshops are held around the country and cost $99 for a day's training.

OTHER POSSIBILITIES

Investigate certification through the National Council on Family Relations (NCFR). The NCFR sponsors the Certified Family Life Educator (CFLE) credential and is the only national program to certify family life educators. The CFLE program encourages applications from all professionals with experience in family life education; minimum requirements are a baccalaureate degree and two years of experience in the field. This certification could open up new doors for you in developing parent and family education programs in your community—perhaps through churches, community colleges, parent-teacher organizations, and local YMCAs and YWCAs.

If you've previously been involved in childbirth or parent education, you may have established a need for other parent or family education programs in your community. For example, mother-daughter, father-son, or grandparenting classes might provide an ideal means of entering into the parent education programs. These can be offered through local churches, hospitals, parent-teacher organizations, or community centers. But beware—these are not for persons without some background in adult and/or child education. In particular, the director of such programs should have a degree in education or be affiliated with a local educational institution.

WHAT'S THE FIRST STEP?

Whether you're going to go all out to lobby your school district to start a program such as PAT or you want to get a program such as Active Parenting under way, you're going to have to get organized. The first step is to establish the need for a parent education program in your community. Active Parenting suggests the following steps:

- *Consider why you want to start your parent education group.* Before trying to sell the idea of parent education to the community, you should be ready to discuss your own reasons for establishing the program and how it will benefit the community. These ideas will help you address potential questions and concerns.

A question you're almost certain to get is why you think your community needs parent education. You may respond by explaining that today, parenting is recognized as a skill and, like any skill, it can be improved with training. The increased incidence of negative phenomena in society over the last few decades—drug and alcohol abuse, teen pregnancy and suicide, widespread violence, and shifts in family status and security—all make the job of effective parenting more difficult than ever. Teamwork is essential to deal with the problems. When parents and educators or community leaders use similar methods, they improve the teamwork. By improving parents' skills, you're improving parent/child relationships; children's behavior in the home, the school, and the community; and even parents' relationships with other adults. Parent education is *that* comprehensive.

- *Enlist the support of community leaders.* Ask the important decision makers in your community for approval and support. Keep in mind the political structure in your community, and follow the established lines of communication. Meet with key players personally. Remember to allow each individual to have ownership in the project; that is, to contribute ideas and to receive credit for them. If persons have the opportunity to affect the program, they will be more likely to support it. You could begin your presentation to potential supporters by showing a video or a promotional brochure of the program. Then, present the parent education plan you've developed, and discuss exactly how that supporter can individually help enact the program. By allowing the supporter to choose a degree of involvement, you'll gain a stronger commitment.

- *Form a committee of persons who can support the program.* Once you win the support of some key players in your community, enlist many types of persons to help you organize, promote, fund, and enact your program. You might try school principals, guidance directors, council leaders, and teachers; social services agency employees; youth court system workers; church education directors; service club leaders; bank officials; or judges.

• *Promote the program.* With local supporters behind your program, you'll next need to reach the people who will benefit from your work. Try these tips for promoting/publicizing:

At such school events as an open house, a school orientation meeting, or parent/teacher conferences, display posters and signup sheets with dates of classes.

Create flyers to hand out to social service agencies, churches, schools, mental health centers, hospitals, youth centers, court system employees, and other institutions.

Present the program to community service clubs.

Provide a written public-service announcement to local radio and television stations and to newspapers.

If you're with a national program such as PAT or Active Parenting, show a preview video to anyone interested.

Send letters and brochures to parents inviting them to sign up.

Call parents you know to be leaders in the community to join your first group.

• *Focus on building leaders who will help promote the program.* Initially, the program needs credibility among parents. The parents of the first program become the community leaders to encourage other parents to get involved in the program.

HOW TO FINANCE THE PROGRAM

Financing for a program such as PAT is generally through school districts; the district itself will be searching for money through federal, state, and local educational funds as well as private grants. For a program such as Active Parenting, finding funding may take abundant research, persistence, and creativity. Yet it may be easier than you think to find funding for local parent education programs. Many organizations in the government and the private sector have set aside money especially for projects such as this. Acquiring the money for the program you wish to develop may involve a somewhat sophisticated grant proposal, or it may require only a letter.

The Active Parenting Program suggests two basic sources of funding: formula grants and competitive grants. *Formula grants* are a set amount of funds that a federal agency gives to a state (the amount of money depends on the number of children or students who will be helped by the program). To qualify for this money, you must submit an application that describes the program. Once your application has been accepted, you must submit a grant proposal. The information you need to put in the proposal is often specified by the grant administrators. Otherwise, you can base your proposal on the many available books on grant proposal writing. *Competitive grants* are offered by public- and private-sector agencies and organizations (such as foundations and corporations) who submit a request for proposals. To acquire these grants, you must write a proposal to prove that your program best meets the grant's criteria.

Ask your local school district if funds are available in the form of grants. The school superintendent or local board of education can tell you about independent, nonprofit foundations that supplement school budgets and that raise money for teacher minigrants and for education programs. You might also call your state school board or department of education for information on state-legislated community foundations. Independent community foundations make small grants to teachers for innovative projects. The Public Education Fund Network (see Resources at the end of the chapter) can help you set up a grant in your community. IMPACT II—The Teacher's Network also provides grants for parent education. Call this organization to see if your school is in one of IMPACT's twenty-six sites in seventeen states.

Don't neglect possible funding by private-sector sources and foundations. Public or private nonprofit agencies often have fixed grants. Local private foundations are your best bet for small grants;

for larger grants, the Council on Foundations (see Resources at the end of the chapter) may suggest appropriate sources.

If you just need enough money to get the parent education up and running, don't forget also to approach such sources as the Rotary Club, Parent-Teacher Organization, Jaycees, Junior League, United Way, and so on.

HOW MUCH DO I CHARGE?

If you're a PAT parent educator, expect to make about $15 per hour. In that program, assuming that you devote approximately twenty hours per week to home visits (including travel time), that comes to about $300 per week.

If you plan on having various sorts of parenting classes through organizations such as Active Parenting, plan on $20 to $30 per couple for a single class or more for a series of two or three classes. If the class is funded through a grant, parents may not be paying; you may be paid through the grant itself. In that case, you may be paid a set fee per class.

WHERE DO I WORK?

That depends on the type of parent education you're pursuing. Are you going to be a PAT parent educator? If you're involved in this or any other program that involves one-on-one interaction with parent and child, much of your work time will be spent in your clients' homes. If you're involved in a program such as Active Parenting, you'll likely be in a classroom, either at a local school, church, or community center. Other parenting skills classes that involve group meetings will likewise take place in a classroom setting.

Parent education gives you an opportunity to improve the life of children beyond your own family. It can also allow flexibility in scheduling, modest financial rewards, and great personal and professional satisfaction. If parent education programs are available in your community, find your place in them. If they're not available, get cracking. There's almost certainly a need.

RESOURCES

BOOK

B. Annye Rothenberg, editor. *Parentmaking: A Practical Handbook for Teaching Parent Classes about Babies and Toddlers.* Menlo Park, CA: Banster Press, 1995.

ORGANIZATIONS

Parents As Teachers National Center, Inc.
10176 Corporate Square Drive
Suite 230
St. Louis, MO 63132
314-432-4330
Fax: 314-432-8963
e-mail: patnc@patnc.org
Will send a folder with brochures, articles, and information on getting a PAT program started in your school district.

Active Parenting Publishers, Inc.
810 Franklin Court
Suite B
Marietta, GA 30067
800-825-0060
Fax: 770-429-0334
e-mail: CService@activeparenting.com
This video-based parent education program provides a wide variety of other parent education materials and has day-long training seminars.

Systematic Training Effectiveness for Parents (STEP)
American Guidance Service (AGS)
4201 Woodland Road
Publishers' Building
Circle Pines, MN 55014
612-786-4343

National Council on Family Relations
3989 Central Avenue NE
Suite 550
Minneapolis, MN 55421
612-781-9331

FUNDING SUPPORT

Public Education Fund Network
202-628-7460
Assists in locating resources for setting up a grant for parent education in your community.

IMPACT II—The Teacher's Network
212-966-5582
Grant support for twenty-six sites in seventeen states.

Goals 2000: Educate America Act
For more information on this new school-improvement act, call the U.S. Department of Education at 800-USA-LEARN.

Council on Foundations
202-466-6512
Information about funding sources and grants.

7

BREAST IS BEST: BREASTFEEDING COUNSELOR OR LACTATION CONSULTANT

What will you do?	Counsel women who want to breastfeed
How many hours a week?	5–40 hours
Your work hours?	Variable; depends on employment situation
Will you need licensing/ certification?	None required, but strongly recommended
What can you earn?	Highly variable; may be voluntary
Liability insurance needed?	No personal insurance required; some employers may provide

When I was an infant, breastfeeding was hardly considered a choice. Going recently through memorabilia, I found the formula recipe my mother's obstetrician had given her for my newborn diet, a concoction that included evaporated milk and corn syrup. It benefited my dentist's pocketbook, if nothing else. But my mother, like most women of her generation, had come to believe that baby formula was the nutritional equivalent of breast milk.

We know better now. More than four decades later, there are dozens of books on breastfeeding, professional and consumer organizations to promote breastfeeding, support groups, and breastfeeding classes. Great strides have been made in educating new parents. Everyone—even formula companies—agrees that breastfeeding is best. But breastfeeding, which may seem like the most natural of human functions, isn't always that easy for all women. To be sure, physiologic issues may come into play; but more common obstacles for the new mother are societal and family pressures. The need has never been greater for breastfeeding counselors. And, while health care professionals with advanced medical degrees should learn more about and should support the breastfeeding mother, the nonmedically trained breastfeeding counselor can provide advice, support, and resources for the woman who wants to breastfeed but needs help getting started. It's a great opportunity for a mother who has breastfed and who wants to help others have a good experience in this most personal and bonding experience.

WHY THE NEED?

Despite increased awareness about the benefits of breastfeeding, knowledge about the how-to's is still lacking. A mother might believe that breastfeeding is the best choice and might be committed to it. But sore nipples during her first few tries or the first few weeks might discourage her from continuing. She may feel a sense of failure unless she gets help. Her husband or her mother or her friends may be pressuring her to bottlefeed. She may feel torn by the need to go back to work. Perhaps she has incorrect information about the effect that breastfeeding will have on her breasts.

She may not be receiving the support for breastfeeding from the medical professionals she has come to trust during her pregnancy. During the last decade, the length of a hospital stay after childbirth has been cut to twenty-four hours or less in many areas. That does not provide much time for hospital personnel to introduce breastfeeding. In earlier times, once the new mom arrived home, at least she would have family support; she cannot count on that any more. Therefore, unless she has resources for breastfeeding help and support, the new mother may simply not have the wherewithal to sustain breastfeeding her newborn.

It doesn't take a medical degree to provide support to women facing these dilemmas. It does take compassion, understanding, empathy, patience, and, of course, some training and knowledge. These traits, if not innate, can all be acquired.

Important Reasons for Breastfeeding

Breastfeeding, like birth, empowers women—not in the conventional, more masculine way that's usually associated with power. It is the power of human closeness that gives quality and meaning to our lives. When a mother breastfeeds, she develops a sense of accomplishment in herself and her abilities. No events are more vital to humanity than childbearing and breastfeeding.

And breastfeeding is healthful for both mother and baby.

Benefits to the baby. Breastfeeding is the most natural and nutritious way to encourage a baby's development. Breast milk is composed of the unique combination of fats, sugars, minerals, proteins, vitamins, and enzymes that optimizes human development. And although formula may provide many of the nutrients a baby needs, it does not contain *colos-*

trum—the perfect starter food for babies. This substance is found in the breast during pregnancy and is the fluid that the baby gets when it first breastfeeds. Colostrum provides baby with an unmatched immunity against bacteria and viruses, and it acts as a natural laxative for clearing baby's intestines, decreasing the chances of jaundice. A few days after baby's birth, mature breast milk replaces the colostrum. The breast milk continues to supply the newborn with antibodies from the mother that give the baby a natural immunity to many common childhood infections and decreases the chances of allergic reactions.

Breastfed babies have fewer ear, respiratory, and intestinal infections. They are less likely to have childhood diabetes and lymphoma. They have fewer learning disabilities. Breastfed babies are one-tenth as likely as those who are not to be admitted to the hospital during the first year. Babies who are exclusively breastfed for at least six months have a reduced risk of cancer before age fifteen. They are less likely to die of sudden infant death syndrome (SIDS), or crib death. Breastfed babies are less likely to become obese because overfeeding is less likely than with bottlefeeding. Breastfeeding offers babies emotional security because the skin-to-skin contact assists in reducing the stress babies experience as they enter the world from the safety of the womb. It also seems to offer better mouth and tooth development for the baby and healthier development of oral muscles and facial bones.

Finally, breast milk is always fresh, clean, just the right temperature, instantly available, and the most nutritious feeding system for the lowest cost.

Benefits to the mother. The ongoing production of milk in

continued

the mother burns calories, helping with weight loss after pregnancy. The milk-producing hormone *prolactin* is a wonderful byproduct of breastfeeding. Called the mothering hormone, prolactin has a relaxing effect on mother and stimulates maternal instincts. Breastfeeding demands lower expenditures of mom's energy than does artificial feeding. Finally, very recent research suggests that women who breastfeed have a reduced risk of premenopausal breast cancer, cervical cancer, and osteoporosis.

Benefits to society. And if all these benefits were not enough (which they should be), there are some very compelling economic incentives to breastfeed. Breastfeeding often results in healthier children, reducing health care costs to society as a whole. James P. Grant of UNICEF points out that exclusive breastfeeding could go a long way toward canceling out the health difference between being born into poverty and being born into affluence. The U.S. National Institute of Environmental Health Sciences estimates that the national infant-mortality rate could be cut nearly in half (from 9 per 1,000 to 5 per 1,000) by making sure that every mother who can breastfeed does breastfeed. And, according to the U.S. Department of Agriculture, "It has been estimated that $29 million could be saved annually in formula costs if WIC (Women, Infants, and Children) mothers would breastfeed for just one month."

WHAT'S THE FIRST STEP?

You can be a resource for new breastfeeding mothers; in fact, the need is urgent. According to an article in *Parenting Magazine* in 1995, despite the growing number of certified lactation consultants, there is still only one consultant for every 761 breastfeeding women. As a result of that article, the International Lactation Consultants Association (ILCA), the main certifying body for lactation consultants, reported that in 1985 (the year ILCA was founded), 259 lactation consultants were certified through their organization; by 1995, 1,559 were certified. (These are international figures; the United States accounts for about two-thirds of the total.) Depending on your current educational background and training, there are several levels of expertise that you may wish to pursue, from serving as a peer counselor for La Leche League International (LLLI) to becoming a certified lactation consultant, or both. The first step is taking stock of your background and then determining how much additional education you'll need—and how much time and training you're willing to invest.

LA LECHE LEAGUE INTERNATIONAL

The Source

Almost anyone interested in breastfeeding is familiar with the pioneering work of LLLI. Founded in 1956 by seven breastfeeding mothers, this organization was developed to give information and encouragement, to all mothers who want to breastfeed their babies, mainly through one mother helping another. Through an ongoing series of four discussion-and-support meetings, LLLI brings together any women interested in breastfeeding. The meetings are led by trained volunteer leaders, who are also available for telephone help. LLLI's book, *The Womanly Art of Breastfeeding*, is a standard, and information sheets on many individual topics are available. A crucial resource for any woman who wants to help breastfeeding mothers, it complements the work of physicians and other health care providers.

LLLI reaches out to health care professionals to encourage breastfeeding, holding physician seminars accredited by the American Medical Association, the American Association of Obstetrics and Gynecology, the American Osteopathic Association, and the American Academy of Pediatrics. It holds Lactation Specialist Workshops as well as continuing education seminars for nurses, LLL leaders, and others who work with breastfeeding mothers.

Becoming a Peer Counselor

Among the programs it has for women who have breastfed, and are interested in helping other women breastfeed, is the La Leche Peer Counselor Program, a training program designed to teach mothers how to help other mothers learn about breastfeeding. The Peer Counselor program is offered in areas where mothers do not have easy access to LLL groups.

Peer counselors are women who want to help mothers from low-income or minority groups or other communities with a low incidence of breastfeeding. The counselor, of course, must be enthusiastic about breastfeeding and must have breastfed at least one baby. She must be recommended by a health care provider or a LLL leader and must complete a breastfeeding training course. She presents breastfeeding information in clinics and provides telephone help to mothers.

The LLLI Peer Counselor Program has trained more than 900 women to help mothers in their communities breastfeed. These mothers have reached more than 30,000 women.

To become a peer counselor, contact the LLLI Outreach Department (see Resources at the end of the chapter). Training for administering LLLI Peer Counselor Workshops are 2.5-day sessions.

BECOMING A LACTATION CONSULTANT

Lactation consultants are allied health care providers who possess the necessary skills, knowledge, and attitudes to facilitate breastfeeding. With a focus on preventive health care, lactation consultants encourage self-care and parental decision-making prenatally and postnatally. Lactation consults also provide a problem-solving resource to provide appropriate information, suggestions, and referrals in a variety of settings, such as hospitals, clinics, physician's offices, and one-on-one with the mother.

Lactation consultants may have a variety of professional backgrounds; no specific educational background is generally required. However, anyone wishing to become a lactation consultant should be willing to meet minimal competencies in the field; this means becoming an International Board-Certified Lactation Consultant (IBCLC). To become an IBCLC, you must take a multihour board certification examination administered by the International Board of Lactation Consultant Examiners (IBLCE), the testing body of ILCA.

TRAINING AND CERTIFICATION

Certification as an IBCLC is intended for persons already experienced in lactation or breastfeeding consultation. Candidates for certification are also required to have extensive practical experience as a breastfeeding consultant before taking the certifying exam. The test covers maternal and infant anatomy, physiology, nutrition, psychology, research, ethical and legal issues, public health implications, and more. Candidates must have either:

- A bachelor's degree or higher, plus a minimum of 2,500 hours of practice as a breastfeeding consultant; they must also have a minimum of thirty hours of continuing education (workshop sessions, conferences, courses, in-service programs for health professionals, volunteer counseling, and so on) specific to breastfeeding within three years immediately before taking the exam, or
- An associate's degree, including a diploma RN or at least two years of post–high school training, plus at least 4,000 hours of practice as a breastfeeding consultant, plus at least thirty hours of continuing education credit specific to breastfeeding within three years immediately before taking the exam.

Courses are available to prepare for the test. These may be available as home study courses. The Breastfeeding Support Consultants' Center for Lactation Education, directed by Judith Lauwers, for example, offers five comprehensive lactation courses, which may carry college credit recommendations. These courses provide training for persons preparing for certification through the International Board of Lactation Consultants and for certified lactation consultants seeking to enhance their skills. These courses vary in cost from $380 to $1,650. There is a one-time $35 application fee and an $85 enrollment fee in addition to tuition.

Lact-Ed, Inc., provides the Lactation Consultant Exam Preparation Course. This five-day intensive course is designed to help the participant identify strengths and weaknesses in knowledge and to prepare to sit the IBLCE certifying exam. The course covers all of the material on the exam and ends with an exam simulation that is one-fourth the length of the actual exam. The course costs about $800.

ASPO/Lamaze, better known for its childbirth education programs, also provides training programs for aspiring lactation consultants and for a wide spectrum of persons who simply support and want to promote breastfeeding. The ASPO/Lamaze Breastfeeding Specialist Program is a two-day workshop designed for (1) childbirth educators who wish to improve their ability to enhance the initiation and duration of breastfeeding through education and counseling of women and their families, (2) perinatal nurses who want to improve their skills in facilitating successful breastfeeding initiations, (3) community-based health professionals who wish to expand their knowledge of specialized breastfeeding support techniques, and (4) family and friends who are motivated to help other women breastfeed. Each participant who completes the workshop will be certified as an ASPO/Lamaze Breastfeeding Support Specialist. Workshops are limited to 100 participants. A schedule is available through ASPO/Lamaze (see Resources at the end of the chapter).

Many state departments of health also provide breastfeeding training courses. The Texas Department of Public Health, for example, offers various courses for peer counselors as well as for physicians.

These courses are often very reasonable, costing only $40 to $60. The length of these courses varies depending on the level of expertise already attained and the level to be acquired. The Missouri Department of Health provides promotional posters, pamphlets, and single-page sheets.

WHERE DO I WORK?

Are you interested in becoming a peer counselor? You may be doing a good portion of your work on the phone at home or at your client's home. Are you going to teach a breastfeeding class? You'll likely be teaching at the local YWCA, community center, women's center, or hospital in an informal classroom environment. Whatever the locale, the crucial component is that the area be private and comfortable—both in terms of seating and temperature.

WHAT SUPPLIES DO I NEED?

What you need to start depends on your circumstances. If you'll be teaching breastfeeding classes, you should have some demonstration materials, such as breast pumps for new mothers working outside the home. You should be able to make appropriate reading materials available. A "lending library" with some of the best LLL publications would be great; at least be able to supply informational brochures (see Resources at the end of the chapter). If you're going to be a peer counselor, you need to invest in few supplies; you should definitely know where appropriate resources can be obtained.

HOW DO I FIND CLIENTS?

Not surprisingly, most clients will come from two main sources: mother's health care providers and word of mouth from former clients. If you are a LLL leader, take advantage of this organization's marketing efforts.

A great way to market your services is by distributing handouts at physicians' offices, clinics, and other health care provider sites. This need not require great writing skills on your part. You can depend on a newsletter such as *LACTNEWS* (published three times a year); it contains timely reports on breastfeeding research in a format attractive to a professional referral base. Your business name and information specific to your local area will be formatted into the basic newsletter. The price of this service, provided by Austin Lactation Associates in Austin, Texas (see Resources at the end of the chapter), varies according to the number of copies requested. *Moms and Babies,* a two-page customized newsletter, is a great way to get your name out to breastfeeding moms and moms-to-be; it provides accurate breastfeeding information in a short, easy-to-read format. It is sold in bulk subscriptions to health care providers, including breastfeeding consultants. Each issue contains articles on topics such as "First Nursings," "SHHhhh—Baby Sleeping!," "What's in It for Me?," and a "Month-by-Month Guide to the Breastfeeding Baby." The newsletter can be customized to contain your own name, address, and services. You can also add information about local news and events of interest to new parents. You will receive a laser-printed master for copying and distribution.

Or be creative. Develop your own FAQ (frequently asked questions) or fact sheet. Be sure to leave enough space to print your name and address and a description of the services you offer.

HOW MUCH DO I CHARGE?

What you charge varies widely. Are you going to "put up your shingle" and provide a private service as a lactation consultant? Check with health care professionals in your area to see what the going rate is; you may also want to check with a variety of insurance companies to find out if women will receive reimbursement for your services. (This may become more commonplace as the trend toward breastfeeding continues to resurge.) As a lactation consultant, you must be certified as a health care professional.

Or you may wish to be associated with a clinic, physician's office, hospital, or managed-care organization for which you will likely receive a salary; your earnings will depend on your training and educational background.

If, on the other hand, you choose to be a LLLI peer counselor, your services will likely be voluntary. As most LLLI volunteers will assure you, however, the gratification that comes from helping new mothers breastfeed is priceless.

OTHER OPPORTUNITIES TO HELP BREASTFEEDING WOMEN

Becoming a Breastfeeding Resource Center

Whether or not you choose to become a peer counselor or to make the professional and financial investment to become a certified lactation consultant, there are other ways in which you can help breastfeeding mothers. One way is to become a Breastfeeding Resource Center (BRC). BRCs act as independent sources of breastfeeding information in areas where there are no accredited LLLI leaders or groups. A BRC can be either an individual interested in promoting breastfeeding in the community (e.g., physician, nurse, lactation consultant, dietitian, childbirth educator) or a part of an organization that provides high-quality breastfeeding materials at a reasonable cost to expectant and new mothers (e.g., public health offices, hospitals, WIC clinics, breastfeeding support groups, and community information centers).

It will cost you $60 to enroll as a BRC through LLLI. In return, you will receive:

- A copy of the famed book *The Womanly Art of Breastfeeding*, published by LLLI.
- A copy of *Breastfeeding Pure and Simple*, LLLI's easy-to-read book for new mothers.
- A one-year subscription to *Breastfeeding Abstracts,* a quarterly newsletter for health care providers that features summaries of recent research, book reviews, and clinical commentaries.
- A Special Circumstances Packet of information sheets on topics that include breastfeeding premature, chronically ill, and adopted babies.
- A collection of ten copies each of breastfeeding-education materials that include information on the most commonly asked questions on breastfeeding management.
- A 15 percent discount on most purchases from the LLLI catalog, which features books on breastfeeding, childbirth, and parenting, as well as other lactation aids at a substantial bulk discount on reorders.
- A discount of $20 when you renew your BRC subscription, plus a special packet of breastfeeding-education materials.

Making yourself available as a BRC may be a way to enhance your visibility in the community as well as to bring in a small source of income. Remember, in the spirit of LLLI, these materials must be made available at low cost.

Selling Breastfeeding Equipment

The LLLI-Medela Breastfeeding-Aid Sales Program offers contact with LLLI who can provide quality breast pumps, supplemental nutrition systems, hand-expression funnels, and breast shells to new and expectant mothers. You can be the resource. It does take some training: you must be thoroughly familiar with all of the equipment yourself. This is available through LLLI courses and seminars. Contact the La Leche League Outreach Department for more information.

Breastfeeding is more than just a method of feeding; it is also a way of caring for and comforting a baby. For many mothers, breastfeeding becomes an integral part of their relationship with their baby. When questions about breastfeeding arise, it is crucial that they be able to resolve them with accurate, reassuring, and authoritative information. A cookbook approach to breastfeeding counseling—where every mother is given the same answer for a given dilemma—won't work. What makes giving breastfeeding help so fascinating and challenging is the creativity it requires to find just the right variation that will work in each unique situation.

If you've breastfed your own children, you know how much support can help. Choose a program or project right for you, and then help to make breastfeeding as enjoyable for mothers and babies as it should be.

RESOURCES

BOOKS AND OTHER PUBLICATIONS

(All of the books listed may be ordered through La Leche League International, 1400 North Meacham Road, Schaumburg, IL 60173, 847-519-7730.)

Breastfeeding Answer Book by Nancy Mohrbacher and Julie Stock. Schaumburg, IL: LLLI, 1997. (Softcover, spiral bound, 455 pages, $52.)
This is a must for all La Leche League leaders, peer counselors, and lactation consultants.

The Womanly Art of Breastfeeding by La Leche League International. Schaumburg, IL: LLLI, 1991. (Softcover, 425 pages, $8.95.)

Lactation: Physiology, Nutrition, and Breast-Feeding, edited by Margaret C. Neville. New York: Plenum, 1983.
This is the one scholarly, scientific book on lactation physiology.

Counseling the Nursing Mother by Judith Lauwers, Candace Woessner, and the CEA of Greater Philadelphia. (Three-ring notebook binder, includes tables and study guides, 527 pages, $36.95.) Garden City, NY: Avery, 1989.

A Practical Guide to Breastfeeding by Jan Riordan, R.N., M.N. Sudbury, MA: Jones and Bartlett, 1990. (Softcover, 383 pages, $22.95.) LLLI publication No. 370.
Written for nurses by an LLLI leader and pediatric nurse.

An Overview of Solutions to Breastfeeding and Sucking Problems by Susan Meintz Maher. ($6.50.) Schaumburg, IL: LLLI, 1988.

Lactation Consultant Series
(8 1/2 by 11 inches, three-hole punched, series price $36.) LLLI publication No. 288-PK.

The Lactation Consultant Series is for anyone who counsels nursing mothers: physicians, nurses, and La Leche League leaders, and professional lactation consultants.

Each unit in the series provides an in-depth discussion of a particular topic, including comprehensive background information, counseling strategies, specific breastfeeding techniques, tips on dealing with other health care providers, and so on.

Topical Outline for Lactation Consultants. ($5) LLLI publication No. 520.
An outline for candidates who seek an overview of the specialty.

Summary of the Lactation Consultants Exam by Leon Gross. ($5) LLLI publication No. 580.
An annual summary of the development and structure of the Lactation Consultant Exam. Please specify by year when ordering.

Breastfeeding Abstracts. LLLI publication No. 192. (Annual subscription $9.50.)
A quarterly newsletter for health professionals that features abstracts of the latest research in lactation and breastfeeding.

Leaven. Bimonthly magazine for LLLI leaders. (Annual subscription $15.)

Clinical Issues in Lactation. Published by the Center for Lactation Education/a division of Breastfeeding Support Consultants (see page 147). (Annual subscription $18; 3 issues.)

Mothering Your Nursing Toddler by Norma Jane Baumgarne. Schaumburg, IL: LLLI, 1982. (Softcover, 208 pages, $7.95.)

Bestfeeding: Getting Breastfeeding Right for You by Mary Renfrew, Chloe Fisher, and Suzanne Arms. Berkeley, CA: Celestial Arts, 1990 (Softcover, 225 pages, $14.95.)

La Leche League Information Sheets: Order a sample series from La Leche, which includes the following publications: *Nutrition and Breastfeeding; Positioning Your Baby at the Breast; Increasing Your Milk; Can Breastfeeding Become the Cultural Norm?; When*

You Breastfeed Your Baby; Practical Hints for Working and Breastfeeding; The Breastfeeding Father; Breastfeeding after Cesarean Birth; Does Breastfeeding Take Too Much Time?

VIDEOTAPE

Breastfeeding Your Baby: A Mother's Guide. Produced by Medela, Inc., in cooperation with LLLI. Schaumburg, IL: LLLI. ($29.95).

ORGANIZATIONS

La Leche League International (LLLI)
1400 North Meacham Road
Schaumburg, IL 60173
847-519-7730
Call for breastfeeding help or for information about local programs. For information on becoming a peer counselor, contact Marijane McEwan in the Outreach Department.

International Lactation Consultants Association (ILCA)
4101 Lake Boone Trail
Suite 201
Riley, NC 27607
919-787-5181
This is the parent organization for the International Board of Lactation Consultant Examiners. Provides information about lactation courses and programs in the United States and Canada and a calendar of when and where they are offered.

International Board of Lactation Consultant Examiners (IBLCE)
P.O. Box 2348
Falls Church, VA 22042-0348
703-560-7330

IBLCE is the examining board for Certified Lactation Consultants. The IBCLC exam is given each year at various locations around the country to qualifying applicants. Contact the IBLCE office for more information and an application.

Lact-Ed, Inc.
c/o Alison Hazelbaker, M.A., IBCLC
6540 Cedarview Court
Dayton, OH 45459
513-438-9458
Provides courses in preparation for IBCLC certifying exam.

National Alliance for Breastfeeding Advocacy/Lactation Association
Office of Educational Services
254 Conant Road
Weston, MA 02193
617-893-3553
Its mission is to protect, support, and promote breastfeeding by raising public awareness of breastfeeding as a public health issue; by watching and promoting local, state, and federal legislation and policy related to breastfeeding and maternal/child health; by issuing positive breastfeeding messages; by countering media discrediting of breastfeeding; by developing grassroots breastfeeding advocacy programs; and by publishing a newsletter and action alerts.

Breastfeeding Support Consultants
Judith Lauwers, B.A., IBCLC, Director
228 Park Lane
Chalfont, PA 18914
215-822-1281
World Wide Web site: http://bsccenter@aol.com
Offers a variety of courses for the breastfeeding support consultant and lactation specialist.

American Society of Psychoprophylaxis in Obstetrics, Inc. (ASPO/ Lamaze)
1200 19th Street
Suite 300
Washington, DC 20036
800-368-4404
e-mail: ASPO@SBA.com

OTHER SERVICES

LACTNEWS for Lactation Consultants
Austin Lactation Associates
1420 West 51st Street
Austin, TX 78756
World Wide Web site: http://bwc.moontower.com

Moms & Babies: A Customized Newsletter for Breastfeeding Moms
Melissa Clark Vickers, M.Ed., IBCLC
2440 Purdy Road
Huntington, TN 38344
901-986-3082

8

THE KISS OF LIFE: INFANT CPR AND INFANT SAFETY INSTRUCTOR

What will you do?	Teach an infant CPR/baby safety course
How many hours a week?	8–24 hours (up to six classes a week)
Your work hours?	Not traditional; evenings and weekends
Will you need licensing/ certification?	From American Heart Association or American Red Cross; essential for infant CPR
What can you earn?	$30–$50 per student, per course, depending on extent of course
Liability insurance needed?	No personal insurance required

MAKING SURE PARENTS AND BABY SURVIVE INFANCY

"Will I ever survive my baby's infancy?" jokes Mary, a hardworking and conscientious first-time mother. "But more important—I'm almost afraid to say this out loud—how can I be sure my child survives her infancy?"

There are no guarantees in life. But there is the "kiss of life"—*cardiopulmonary resuscitation*, or CPR. It is but one component of a safety training program that is truly essential for every concerned parent. With several hours of study and training, you can be the valuable resource to teach infant CPR and other aspects of infant safety to parents and caregivers.

INFANT CPR/INFANT SAFETY CLASSES

Parents inevitably have to cope with a variety of accidents as their children grow up. Generally, these are minor. But all responsible parents must prepare for the unexpected, especially for catastrophic accidents. To do so, they should know both CPR and the basic first-aid techniques necessary to deal with accidents quickly, effectively, and calmly. The first emergency medical system is in the home.

While the big accidents are less likely, the statistics show that they do happen. Nine thousand children a year in the United States have heart attacks, according to the American Heart Association. Thousands more choke. While phoning for help is a critical first step, the time between the call for help and the arrival of the help may be crucial. It is during that time that lifesaving steps can make the difference. If you become an infant CPR/safety instructor, with certification provided by the American Red Cross or the American Heart Association, you can be the one to help parents become prepared.

You will need to put in some classroom time and some preparation. And you won't make a million dollars doing this; few jobs will make you a million dollars. But if you're already a childbirth educator, you will have a valuable add-on to other childbirth/parent education offerings. If you're not an educator, but you appreciate the importance of infant safety and can commit to several hours' training and more hours of practice, here's a great new opportunity for you.

What Is CPR?

The heart must constantly pump oxygen-rich blood received from the lungs to all organs and tissues of the body. In order for blood to be transported through the circulatory system, a three-part process must be in perfect sync: The airway must be open so that oxygen can enter the lungs; the lungs must supply the oxygen to the blood on its way to the heart; and the heart must pump this oxygen-rich blood through the blood vessels, which deliver it to all of the tissues of the body, including the brain.

This amazingly efficient system continues over a lifetime; it is not often that an infant or a child experiences difficulty with this process, except in the case of accident. But if any portion of this system is disturbed, it can mean big trouble. If the brain is deprived of oxygen-rich blood from the heart because of, say, a heart attack, for more than three minutes, it will start to fail, and brain damage may result. If the heart is deprived of oxygenated blood from the lungs, as in drowning or choking, the victim will die—in as little as eight to twelve minutes—unless emergency action is taken. It is when the circulatory system shuts down—when the heart stops circulating blood and the victim cannot breathe and, therefore, becomes unconscious—that CPR can save a life.

When you perform CPR, you use your hands on the

surface of the chest to artificially pump for the heart; you perform mouth-to-mouth breathing to supply the lungs with oxygen. The result is that you temporarily supply the circulation with oxygen-rich blood to keep the body's vital systems working.

In learning CPR in its simplest form, for either adults or infants, you'll learn the vital ABCs:

A is for *airway*. The person giving CPR opens the victim's mouth, looks in the mouth, and checks the airway for obstructions. The airway is kept open by tilting the child's head back.

B is for *breathing*. If the victim shows no signs of breathing, artificial respiration is required.

C is for *circulation*. Check for a pulse. If a pulse is not present or only very faint and the child is not breathing, CPR is essential—compressions along with artificial respiration.

Knowing the ABCs of CPR can save a life until more sophisticated medical care is available.

WHAT WILL I BE TEACHING?

Either the American Red Cross or the American Heart Association will likely welcome your services as a certified instructor. There is little leeway in what you teach or how you will teach their courses; you must teach a class that meets well-defined national standards. But to make a course offering of infant CPR even more useful, why not turn it into a more comprehensive infant safety course? This would include training in infant CPR and also other aspects of infant safety, such as babyproofing and accident prevention.

You'll teach the 3 Ps—*P*revent, *P*repare, and *P*ractice—to parents and other caregivers in order to make the home the safest haven possible. A typical infant CPR/infant safety course might include information about the following emergencies:

Everyday first aid

As a child grows, she inevitably experiences commonplace accidents such as cuts, bruises, blisters, bites, and stings. Most of the time, these are minor injuries that can be treated at home. But differentiating major from minor injuries—and acting appropriately in either case—is crucial. That's what you'll be teaching.

Choking

If a child's airway becomes completely blocked, whether by a piece of food, gum, or a small toy, help can be as simple as patting an infant on the back. Sometimes, however, more serious action may be necessary, including, in an older child, the Heimlich maneuver. You'll be teaching parents how to perform back blows, chest thrusts, and the Heimlich maneuver—abdominal thrusts designed to dislodge objects that block the airway.

Shock

Shock refers to a dangerous drop in the flow of oxygen to organs and tissues due to a precipitous decrease in blood pressure, made worse by fear or pain. If it is not dealt with quickly, the vital organs may stop functioning. You will help the parents recognize the signs of shock, teach them how and when to get outside help, and alert them to when CPR is needed.

Drowning

A child can drown in as little as two inches of water. You will emphasize to your clients the importance of never leaving the child unattended near a wading or swimming pool, a bathtub, or even a bucket of water. If their preventive efforts fail, however, you'll teach them how to rescue the child, checking for breathing, airway, and pulse, and when CPR should be administered.

Electric shock

You will teach about avoiding hazards such as exposed and/or frayed cords. In severe shocks, the child may lose consciousness; CPR may become necessary. You will teach how to break contact with the source, how to examine the child for burns, and how to monitor the child's condition.

Sudden infant death syndrome

Sudden infant death syndrome (SIDS) is every parent's worst nightmare. You can teach the most recent guidelines on avoiding SIDS and what to do if, for any reason, baby should stop breathing. Parents can learn how to use monitoring equipment if their child is at high risk of SIDS.

Bleeding

Cuts and bruises are usually not serious and can be dealt with at home. Some cuts will require stitches. Severe bleeding—either internal or external—can lead to shock and, eventually, to loss of consciousness. You will teach parents how to stop or minimize the bleeding if the wound is external, including how to apply a tourniquet. You will also instruct them on how to spot signs of internal bleeding. You will teach them how to treat for shock and the importance of getting help immediately.

Head injuries

If a child bangs or knocks his head and does not recover within a few minutes, there may be reason for concern. Head injuries that may be serious include those that produce severe bleeding or that result in symptoms of concussion, even several hours after the injury. You will teach parents how to recognize the symptoms of concussion or skull fracture and what to do if the child is unconscious or bleeding.

Seizures and convulsions

Convulsions may result from high fever, epilepsy, head injuries, diseases that damage the brain, and poisoning. They may occur for no obvious reason. Convulsions are a sign of a disturbance in the normal electrical impulses in the brain, causing muscles to jerk involuntarily. They are disturbing to both the infant and the parents. You will teach parents the signs of various types of convulsions (such as "grand mal" and "petit mal"), the importance of not trying to restrain a child during a seizure, and proper procedures before medical help is available.

Burns and scalds

The severity of a burn is defined by the amount of damage to the skin: superficial, or *first-degree*, burns, may be caused by spilling a hot liquid or touching a very hot surface, such as a stove. Partial-thickness, or *second-degree*, burns are more serious and result in blistering of the skin. Full-thickness, or *third-degree*, burns, damage all layers of the skin. Third-degree burns may result in fluid loss due to weeping of the skin and in damage to the nerves and muscles. You'll teach your clients how to dress a minor burn; what to do with a major burn after calling 911; how to monitor for shock; what to do if a child's clothes catch on fire; and what not to do, such as touch the affected area, dress a serious burn, apply lotions, or overcool the child.

Poisoning

Every household contains poisons, which, for a child, include medicines, bleach, weed killers, and certain plants and fungi. You will teach parents to recognize the poisons, including those that may not be so obvious. Then, you'll tell them how to baby proof the house to make most poisons inaccessible. But you will also teach them if, despite their conscientious efforts and supervision, baby swallows a poison, what they should do, including immediately calling the poison control center and inducing vomiting (if that is advised by the poison control center).

Eye injuries

Common reasons for eye injuries are a foreign body or chemical in the eye, a blow to the eye causing bruising or a black eye, or a cut in or near the eye. Any such injury should be taken seriously, and the child should usually be taken to the emergency room.

You'll teach the parents how to spot an eye injury that may not be so obvious, how to flush the eye of a foreign object or substance, and what to do if there is a blow to the eye (from a baseball or bat, for example).

Nose injuries

A bloody nose may seem like a minor childhood injury, but there are times when it can be a sign of something more serious. You'll teach parents how to handle a simple nosebleed, how to recognize when it's something more serious (perhaps a sign of a skull fracture), and what to do if air flow is impaired.

Stings and bites

Stings and bites are a part of every childhood. Usually, they're not serious, and the discomfort passes quickly. But they can lead to infection at the puncture site or to allergic reactions. A bite from a tick could lead to Lyme disease. You'll teach parents how to remove stingers and ticks, how to recognize and what to do in the case of an allergic reaction, and what to do to relieve discomfort.

Tooth trauma

Those two front teeth that beginning walkers and tripping toddlers always seem to hit are remarkably resilient. Often, if they're loosened, they spring back and continue to survive—even through more falls. But loose teeth can be more serious, and you'll teach parents when to consult a dentist and what to do if the gums and mouth are bleeding.

Fractures, dislocations, strains, and sprains

The most common type of childhood fracture is a *greenstick fracture*—the bone bends and only partially breaks. Other types include a *simple fracture*, or clean break, and a *compound fracture*—the broken bone breaks through the skin. A dislocation is a bone that is displaced from its joint, usually after a wrenching force. First, you'll teach your students the acronym *ICES* for care of common strains, sprains, and fractures: *I*ce, *C*ompression, *E*levation, and *S*upport. You'll also teach them how to recognize a fracture or a dislocation, how to differentiate between a sprain or a strain, and how to tie a sling. If a spinal or neck fracture is suspected, emphasize the importance of not moving the child.

TRAINING AND CERTIFICATION

Certification is essential, both for learning and for teaching infant CPR and first aid. In the United States, two organizations provide training in adult and infant CPR: the American Heart Association and the American Red Cross. More than 5 million persons each year receive CPR training from instructors taught by the American Heart Association or American Red Cross. Check with your local chapter or affiliate of either organization to find out about taking a class. These classes will include training in basic first aid and in the Heimlich maneuver. Upon completing a CPR course, you will then receive certification in some aspect of basic life support. After learning the technique, you will need to take additional training to become a certified infant CPR/first aid instructor.

Because the technique for infant CPR is somewhat different from that for adults, this technique may be taught in a separate class, or it may be a part of a class series including both infant and adult CPR.

Learning Infant CPR

The American Red Cross offers certification as a First Aid and Safety Instructor, Community CPR Instructor, or American Red Cross Infant and Child CPR Instructor. The American Heart Association provides similar courses in many areas. Their four- to six-hour Heart Saver A course is more geared toward adult CPR, but includes critical information on the physiologic basis of CPR: why it works and how it works. More relevant is their six-hour Heart Saver B course, which covers material covered in the Heart Saver A course and then teaches procedures for single-rescuer infant-child CPR. It details the differences among adults, children, and infants when using CPR and explains where and how the CPR procedures for each differ.

An infant-child CPR class will typically train parents and caregivers to overcome reluctance to act in emergency situations and to recognize and care for life-threatening respiratory or cardiac emergencies in infants and children. Almost always, basic first aid instruction is included. The objectives are to:

- Identify how to reduce the risk of injury to infants and children.
- Learn how to care for an infant or child who stops breathing or who is choking and to learn how to give CPR to an infant or child who is unconscious and whose heart has stopped beating.
- Identify how to use the community's emergency medical services system effectively.

The suggested class length is about five hours, and the cost is usually about $50. Upon completing the skills outline in the course and passing a written examination with a minimum score of 80 percent, you will be certified in infant-child CPR. This certification is good for one year only and must be renewed at a refresher course. Participant materials required typically include the American Red Cross Infant and Child CPR participant's manual.

Becoming an Instructor

The American Red Cross instructors' course provides training and practical experience to become certified as Community First Aid and CPR Instructors (see course outline at the end of the chapter). The six-hour American Red Cross Instructor Candidate Training (ICT), which costs $20, is a prerequisite for all instructor courses. Then, the instructor candidate proceeds to a five-hour Instructor Pre-Course Testing Session, which will cost $30. Within ninety days, the student must then complete the Community First Aid and Safety Instructor Course, which costs $80.

These courses require some texts, all available through the Red Cross: The *Community and First Aid Safety—Student Manual*; *First AID and CPR Instructor's Manual*; and *Instructor Candidate Training Manual.* Many courses will require that you bring additional supplies, such as triangular bandages, gauze, or other dressings; in other courses, these will be supplied for you.

The American Heart Association Heart Saver courses also have special sessions for instructor training, with fees similar to those of the Red Cross. Call your local Heart Association for more information.

Remember, you will need to be recertified in CPR every year. This is required for two main reasons: to maintain your skills and to keep up-to-date in new guidelines. For example, in 1992, the American Heart Association and American Red Cross adopted new CPR guidelines that serve as the basis for teaching CPR. These new guidelines recommend:

- In adults, accessing the emergency medical system (EMS) by calling 911 or its equivalent *before* beginning CPR.
- In children, accessing EMS after one minute of CPR.
- Simplified, more consistent protocols for both children and adults.
- Addition of the *recovery position* (rolling the victim on his or her side) to all protocols for victims who are breathing effectively on their own or who resume effective breathing at any time during the delivery of resuscitation efforts.
- Repositioning the victim's head after each unsuccessful attempt to ventilate, before reattempting ventilation.

The new guidelines have been developed to improve the chances of recovery and to simplify teaching CPR skills.

HOW DO I FIND CLIENTS?

Are you a childbirth or parent educator? If so, you have an immediate and, likely, receptive source of clients. Distribute informational brochures in your childbirth education classes.

If you're affiliated with a hospital, be sure to use the publicity and public relations units therein. Infant CPR/infant safety courses, reasonably priced, are a great way to bring new clients to the hospital.

Whether or not you're associated with a hospital, make sure that local pediatricians know about your classes. Give them informational brochures and class schedules that they can distribute to their patients or at least place in waiting rooms. New parents can be recruited during well-child visits and via follow-up telephone calls with new parents and those who seem to call the office frequently.

Your local church or synagogue may be a great resource not

only for getting the word out, but for giving the classes. Also, check with your local YMCA or YWCA to see if they offer classes. If they do, offer your services; if they don't, offer to develop a program. Check with the continuing education office of local community colleges and medical centers to determine if they have infant CPR/infant safety courses or if they would be interested in starting them.

Use local parenting magazines and newspapers to publicize programs. Infant CPR could make a great public interest story. Make yourself available for interviews on local radio stations or television shows to talk about infant safety.

Finally, go to the American Heart Association and the American Red Cross to offer your services to the agencies that just trained you. You may start out as a volunteer, teaching courses more restricted to CPR; but that will help you know if you want to expand your services to more comprehensive classes on infant safety.

Word of mouth is, as always, a great way to get clients. Young parents who have completed a course they consider worthwhile will talk about it to other young couples who are expecting or just had a baby.

WHERE DO I WORK?

A place to give the class is the first and most important consideration. For discussion and demonstration, you'll likely want a classroom-style setup or chairs in a semicircle. But for demonstration of CPR and a variety of other safety procedures, you'll need plenty of room, including open floor space—in a gym, church basement, community center, or open classroom. You'll want to keep the classes quite small—not more than eight to ten students or perhaps five couples per class. A team approach is encouraged: You may well want to teach with another instructor so that one can demonstrate while the other talks. Also, CPR is generally administered by one person or by two persons; certification requires that both techniques be taught.

WHAT SUPPLIES WILL I NEED?

Both infant and adult CPR training requires a specially constructed mannequin on which to practice technique. These are supplied by the Red Cross or the Heart Association. You will also need a first aid kit to demonstrate what should be included, plus a variety of safety devices. You'll want to distribute safety information (such as a reprint of the Preventing Injuries chart at the end of the chapter) for the parents to take home, including a CPR manual and a sheet with important information about local emergency medical services. Be certain that your name and phone number appear on or accompanies all safety literature you distribute. You'll need safety devices such as electrical outlet covers and childproof cabinet locks when discussing accident prevention. Give them a supply of "Mr. Yuk" stickers, available from the U.S. Consumer Products Safety Commission (see Resources at the end of the chapter).

HOW MUCH DO I CHARGE?

The local Red Cross or Heart Association likely sets a standard fee for infant CPR/first aid classes. If you're volunteering for them, this course, which is likely an afternoon or morning session, will likely cost each participant about $30. You may or may not be reimbursed for travel or other expenses, but you will not receive a per student or class fee.

If, however, you're offering a more comprehensive infant CPR/infant safety course, a $50 fee might be appropriate. This fee will include the cost of educational materials, handouts, and so on, for two classes: one devoted to infant CPR and the Heimlich maneuver, and the other for first aid and emergencies.

Infant CPR/infant safety classes can be a delight to teach. Your students will, for the most part, be highly motivated young parents or parents-to-be who are truly looking to be the best parents that they can be. Or they may be concerned grandparents trying to ensure the healthiest, happiest childhood for their new grandchild. Or they may be concerned day-care providers. It's hard to imagine anything more gratifying than educating these caring caregivers in how to best provide a safe environment—and, when the worst happens, how to save a life. The fee you'll be able to collect for this service is small—but the gratification you'll feel is priceless.

INSTRUCTOR TRAINING COURSE OUTLINE

I. Instructor Candidate Training

A. Students and the learning process

B. Effective instruction

C. Conducting a course

D. Evaluations, records, and reports

E. Representing the Red Cross

Candidate must complete a written exam on this section

II. First Aid and CPR Instructor Training

A. Course design

B. Course prerequisites

C. Course preparation

D. Practice teaching session

Candidate must complete a written exam on this section

III. Community First Aid and Safety Certification

A. Deciding to act

B. Emergency action steps

C. Victim assessment

D. Adult airway management

E. Adult CPR

F. Child airway management

G. Child CPR

H. Infant airway management

Candidate must complete a skills practical and a written exam.

I. Injuries

J. Cuts, scrapes, and bruises

K. Burns

L. Muscle, bone, joint injuries

M. Sudden illness

N. Poisoning

O. Heat/cold emergencies

P. Young/elderly victims

Student presentations: Lecture/demonstration

IV. Final Written Exam

Preventing Injuries to Infants—Important Pointers for Your Students

	0–5 months	*6–12 months*
Choking, suffocation	Don't sprinkle baby powder directly on baby—apply with hands. Close container after use. Don't cover mattress with plastic. Don't use pillows. Baby should not sleep with jewelry or pacifier on string. Keep deep-suction bulb handy. Don't leave baby alone in bath. Don't use old cribs that don't meet safety guidelines.	Keep all plastic bags and balloons away from baby. Keep buttons, beads, pennies, and other small objects out of baby's reach. Check toys for removable parts. Don't feed babies raw carrots, nuts, popcorn, hot dogs, and so on. Keep drapery and miniblind cords out of reach, cut ends so there is no loop. Don't leave baby alone in bath. Don't clothe baby in anything with drawstring at the neck.
Falls	Never leave baby on any raised surface. When in doubt, use the floor. Always use strap for infant seat and swing. Keep side rails up on crib.	Lower crib mattress and remove large toys so baby can't build a hill and climb out. Keep walkers away from stairs. Use mesh gates. Use high chair with wide base and locking tray and strap.
Burns	Install smoke detectors on every floor and test monthly. Use only flame-retardant sleepwear. Use sun screen. Lower water heater temperature to below 130°. Never pour or drink hot liquids while holding baby.	Never pour or drink hot liquids while holding baby. Keep hanging cords and table cloths out of reach. Keep baby away from open oven doors. Use plastic outlet covers. Place guards in front of heater or fireplaces.
Accidents	Never leave baby alone in parked car—she could become overheated in hot weather very quickly. Always use rear-facing approved car seat in the back seat.	Keep baby away from all medicines and cleaning supplies. Use childproof cabinet locks. Assume baby will eat anything. Keep bottle of ipecac and emergency telephone numbers handy.

RESOURCES

BOOKS

The American Medical Association Handbook of First Aid and Emergency Care by Stanley M. Zydlo Jr. and James A. Hill. New York: Random House, 1990.

The American Red Cross First Aid and Safety Handbook by the American Red Cross and Kathleen Hanal, M.D. Boston: Little, Brown, 1990.

VIDEOTAPES

Both videos are available from ActivVideo, 815 West Armitage, Suite 220, Chicago, IL 60614; phone 800-333-0901.

Baby Alive. 60 minutes, 1988.
Prepared by the American Academy of Pediatrics, this video shows step-by-step management of the most common infant and childhood emergencies.

Emergency Action. 30 minutes, 1988.
Lifesaving techniques for the whole family.

ORGANIZATIONS

American Heart Association
7272 Greenville Avenue
Dallas, TX 75231
214-706-1330
Call for information about your local affiliate or chapter.

American Red Cross
8111 Galehouse Road
Falls Church, VA 22042
Call your local chapter for information about CPR and infant safety.

SUPPLIES AND CATALOGS

Childbirth Graphics
P. O. Box 21027
Waco, TX 76702-1207
800-299-3366
World Wide Web site: http://www.wrsgroup.com
A complete catalog of teaching aids for birth, sex, and parenting education.

9

THE POWER OF TOUCH: MASSAGE THERAPIST

What will you do?	Train parents in infant massage and teach birthing partners massage techniques
How many hours per week?	1–40 hours
Your work hours?	Variable; not necessarily conventional hours
Will you need licensing/ certification?	Essential in most states for both infant and pregnancy massage; highly recommended regardless of state requirements
What can you earn?	$30–$50 per hour, depending on services and, for infant massage, class size
Liability insurance needed?	Check state requirements

During labor, baby experiences the first massage. Mother's contractions stimulate the child's skin, which sends messages to the nervous system and then the lungs. The purpose? To help baby prepare for the first task after birth: breathing. And even babies born by cesarean section, who might miss this first massage, may receive some benefits of massage from mother. Watch a pregnant woman. She'll often rub and stroke her belly, as if already communicating with her infant through the power of touch. This unconscious massaging may be an early form of bonding.

A CAREER IN MASSAGE THERAPY

Why not help mother and child continue this beautiful and natural way of bonding after birth? And why not bring it full cycle, helping the expectant or new mother enjoy massage as she brings new life into the world?

Massage therapy can be a fulfilling career opportunity. You can help the expectant mom, new mom, and infant learn to relax and enjoy the well-documented health benefits of massage, and you can make money in the process. The infant massage instructor will help new parents learn to bond with their infants by teaching them to communicate through touch. The mother massage therapist will help relieve many of the discomforts of the pregnancy/postpartum period for the expectant or new mom and will help reduce stress and promote general well-being. The mother massage therapist can share some of her techniques with the new father or grandmother or friend to continue the benefits.

These opportunities in massage therapy are particularly appealing to the woman who is social, who wants to set her own hours, and who feels comfortable with providing relaxation and comfort through this very personal art and science of touch.

Massage therapy has enjoyed increased popularity in the last decade or so in this country; but massage is actually an ancient art.

Why the revival? After decades of the medicalization of birth, women have returned to more natural forms of relieving the discomforts of pregnancy and childbirth and their child's discomforts. And fathers are no longer shut out of the birth experience. Now, they may play an active role in birthing their child. One way in which they can comfort the mom is through labor massage.

While infant massage and mother massage may seem to be related fields—and they both provide many of the same benefits for infant and mother—the techniques vary, and training and licensing is very different. For this reason, the opportunities and requirements for each are described separately in this chapter.

INFANT MASSAGE

Linda Wilson, an infant massage instructor in a small town outside of Peoria, Illinois, recently wrote an article entitled, "Will It Play in Peoria?" While a popular perception of infant massage therapy might be that it is New Age, Linda points out that some techniques of infant massage are as old as many cultures themselves. In some parts of India, for example, expectant mothers massage their abdomen several times a day as they softly rock, coo, and sing songs of infancy passed down through thousands of years from mother to daughter. Other women in the family massage the pregnant woman all during pregnancy and labor and for weeks after delivery. In Bali, infants are regarded as holy, having just emerged into life from the spiritual realm. Besides being massaged for the first six months of their lives, infants are carried about so that they have no contact with the "impure earth."

Benefits of Infant Massage

In the United States, the approach to massage has been less spiritual and tradition-based and more scientific. Infant massage has myriad documented psychological and physiologic benefits.

Among the physiologic benefits, infant massage can:

- Strengthen and regulate respiratory, circulatory, and gastrointestinal functions
- Improve muscle tone and motor skills
- Soothe and stimulate the developing sensory and motor nerves
- Stimulate the growing brain cells, influencing mental growth and development
- Help to heal the effects of birth trauma by soothing strained or pulled muscles
- Enhance the infant's sense of touch
- Relieve stress that builds up daily from new encounters with the world, and teach baby to relax
- Relieve gas pain from colic

Psychologically, infant massage can:

- Enhance and nurture the parent-infant relationship and promote bonding
- Teach the baby that his or her needs will be met
- Promote a health body awareness and confident self-image
- Give parents an opportunity to relax and tune in to their infants and develop confidence as caregivers

Babies with special needs can benefit as much as, if not more than, normal babies. For example, preterm infants can benefit from tactile and kinesthetic stimulation. Dr. Tiffany Field, a child psychologist at the University of Miami Medical School, has conducted extensive research in this area. One of her studies included a treatment group of twenty infants with an average weight of three pounds and average gestational age of seven months. They were massaged for fifteen minutes, three times a day for ten consecutive days. The results were dramatic: The treatment group gained 47 percent more weight than a control group of preterm infants who were not massaged. The massaged babies were more alert and scored higher on the Brazelton Neonatal Behavior Assessment Test, a standard test of newborn behavior. They were discharged six days earlier from the hospital, at an average savings of $3,000 per infant. Even after eight months, these infants showed better test results of mental and motor abilities and held on to their advantage in weight over the infants in the study who were not massaged.

Massage can also improve the relationship between parents and preterm babies. Preterm, low-birthweight infants often fail to thrive in the first months of life, often because parents and infant are separated and therefore cannot connect or bond. Parents may feel as if they are taking a tiny stranger—or even an intruder—home from the hospital because they have had so little opportunity to interact. Infant massage promotes the bonding that may have been more difficult to establish with the preterm baby.

Other special-needs infants—those with mental, visual, hearing, or developmental impairments—can also benefit from massage. Parents of such infants are often faced with overwhelming challenges from birth. Often, some of the normal reciprocal interaction that facilitates bonding is not possible because of the infant's handicap. Infant massage tailored to the infant's special needs can communicate love through touch. Other recent studies have shown the benefits of infant massage in cocaine-impaired babies.

Research also indicates that certain brain chemicals called *catecholamines* are enhanced by massage. Many hospital nurseries are incorporating programs that encourage parents, staff, and trained volunteers to hold, touch, and massage infants, particularly those with special needs, such as preemies.

So not only are there tangible benefits to massage in both normal and special needs babies, there are many intangibles as well. Infant massage can become an exchange of love and energy. It can become the cornerstone of trust and love. Parents learn to unwind and relax as they help their babies relax. Parents are also better able to interpret their child's moods, feelings, and needs. These benefits may not be immediately apparent; they may accrue much later in life. Recent studies of adults who have a fear of touch, poor body image, lack of body awareness, high levels of tension, and relationships that lack trust and intimacy reveal that these difficulties often seemed to stem from infancy and childhood experiences. These problems have been found to reflect a lack of nurturing touch and relaxation skills during childhood, high levels of stress, and insecure attachment bonds.

Infant Massage Techniques

The components of the baby massage routine comprise Swedish massage, Indian techniques, and reflexology. Each serves a specific purpose: Swedish massage includes strokes that move toward the heart from the extremities of the body to increase and improve circulation, especially venous and lymphatic flow, while helping to tone muscles. Indian massage techniques do just the opposite, working from the trunk of the body toward the extremities—for example, from the shoulder toward the hand or the upper thigh toward the foot. Indian massage helps relax flexor muscles while balancing and releasing energy. Reflexology, which involves massaging and pressing with thumbs all over the soles of the feet, is believed to help remove toxins from the body, aiding in achieving balance and optimal health.

The infant massage instructor teaches expectant parents, new parents, and caregivers not just a massage technique, but a whole new process of relating to their infants through first learning to relax themselves through stretching, specific breathing, and visualization techniques. Childbirth educators who become infant massage instructors will be able to draw on the relaxation techniques they have taught expectant parents.

The massage instructor also helps the parents communicate with the baby. Eye contact, verbal cues, and close observation as well as actively listening to infants set the pace for the massage. A basic procedure and massage strokes are taught to parents, with instructions to work according to the infant's response. Infants may enjoy massage in one area more than another or may want a shorter or longer session than the time before.

In preparing for an infant massage session, the instructor teaches new parents a few guidelines:

- Find a good time when interruptions are not likely.
- Massage the baby in a warm, comfortable area of the house.
- Play soft music or sing your own special songs to the baby.
- Use *cold pressed* oils. These oils have been extracted only by the use of pressure, not by heat or chemical solvents, which change the characteristics of the oil. Almond, olive, peanut, safflower, avocado, and sunflower oils, all available at most grocery stores, are fine; whatever the preference, it's important to use edible oils, which are nourishing for the skin and safe for the baby if she puts oil-covered fists into her mouth.

Experienced infant massage instructors stress the importance of asking baby's permission before beginning the massage. In Swedish massage, the "hello" stroke is a very light stroke that glides over the body without pressure. After the first few sessions, this will become a cue to the baby, who will let you know whether to continue. If baby seems upset, the massage should be postponed. Infants are often more receptive to having legs and feet worked with first because, at this early stage of development, these are the least vulnerable parts of the body. The massage continues with the abdomen, chest, arms and hands, face, and back. Most strokes are repeated two or three times. In infants younger than one year, passive exercises are done also. This is a sample sequence, of course; the massage may be tailored to each baby's needs. Some sequences might be especially helpful when the baby is teething, congested, or suffering from colic (see box, page 182).

The massage need not end when infants become toddlers. As a baby grows, that special relationship that massage promotes can remain an important source of nurturing and love. Touch relaxation, which helps infants learn to relax their own bodies, in much the same way an expectant mother learns to relax in her childbirth preparation classes, can be beneficial. This is a skill parents can incorporate into their own lives as they try to deal with the stresses of modern living.

What's the First Step?

Infant massage therapists and trainers come from a wide range of backgrounds, and infant massage can be learned by anyone interested in having a loving relationship with babies. You need not have a specific educational background, and licensing, if it exists at all, varies widely from state to state (as it does for adult massage). However, anyone interested in becoming an infant massage instructor should contact the International Association of Infant Massage (IAIM). This is the only organization that has Infant Massage Certification Training; it is also an excellent source of massage supplies and educational materials for both parent and instructor.

Training and Certification

Certification involves:

- Attending a four-day Infant Massage Certification Training workshop
- Completing required reading before, during, or after the training. Required reading includes (1) *Infant Massage: A Handbook for*

Loving Parents (received at the training session), (2) *Infant Massage Instructor's Manual* (received at the training session), and (3) *The Baby Book* by William and Martha Sears, and *Touching* by Ashley Montagu.

- Completing the open-book examination. (The examination study is to be mailed to the trainer within an agreed time frame; most participants need about a week to complete the study.)
- Teaching infant massage classes and obtaining five written evaluations from parents. (This can be done as one class series of five sessions, or five individual classes of three sessions each, or a combination. These evaluations are mailed in with the written examination.)

After the training course, you will receive a complimentary IAIM membership, good until the end of that membership year. This membership can be renewed for one year, or, upon completion of the certification requirements as listed, the membership will be changed to Certified Infant Massage Instructor (CIMI). Thereafter, the annual membership fee is $48. Contact the IAIM (see Resources at the end of the chapter) for information regarding local instructors and instructor training.

Where Do I Work?

After certification, instructors work in many capacities with parents and infants. They teach parent baby courses in various settings, including community/parent education centers, hospitals, teen programs, foster care, and recovery programs. Instructors may also conduct in-service courses and demonstrations for professional groups and conferences. Of course, private instruction to parents may be arranged. Massage sessions with the infants, with you performing the massage, are another possibility, although your focus should be on encouraging the parents to bond with their baby.

How Much Do I Charge?

If you actually perform infant massage yourself, $30 to $50 an hour is a reasonable rate. However, your primary focus will almost certainly be on teaching the massage techniques to parents or perhaps grandparents. This would likely take place in a series of classes—perhaps four weekly sessions of two hours each. Each session might cost the clients $10 per class.

What Supplies Will I Need?

A variety of massage oils are a basic supply, of course. The oils should be stored in spillproof plastic bottles to avoid accidents. Advise parents to schedule a class at a time when baby is generally alert and happy. Parents should also bring towels, and remind them to bring extra diapers for cleaning up and rediapering baby. The only other essentials are a clean, warm, draft-free room and relaxing music to set the mood.

Where Do I Find Clients?

If you're a childbirth educator or doula, chances are you already have valuable contacts. Advertise through childbirth education classes in your area and in local parenting magazines. Offer to speak at childbirth education classes and demonstrate massage techniques. Be sure to bring along business cards and informational brochures. If you're already a childbirth educator, let your clients know of your availability as an infant massage instructor. If you're hospital-based, propose infant massage classes as one of your facility's childbirth education offerings.

Word of mouth may be your best advertising and marketing tool. Satisfied parents who have seen firsthand the benefits of massage will often be more than happy to tell their friends and family about your services.

A Healing Touch: One Mother's Story

"I had tried everything to relieve my Emily's colic," said Jean, a new mother. "Warm baths helped, but only while she was in the water—and she couldn't spend her entire infancy there! I tried to massage her tummy in the water. She liked that. After her bath, I found that massaging her thighs helped. I would slather avocado oil on my hands and, starting with her feet, would work my way up each leg. When I reached her thighs, her wails of despair turned into laughter. Having found what worked, I started to massage her thighs whenever a colicky period began. Even without the bath, her response was always the same.

"The thigh massage the infant massage instructor had shown me went like this. I would lay Emily in my lap on her back with her head on my knees and her feet at my stomach. I would then place a hand on each thigh, thumb in the groin area and fingers on the outside of the leg. Then I would use a firm, deep kneading motion with equal pressure on the inside and the outside of the leg, squeezing, rolling, then releasing. It worked every time—at least until the next colic bout! You see, massage was not the cure-all for Emily's colic. But it was a really helpful way for her to get relief from her discomforts—and for me and her dad to get relief, however temporary, from her crying! And it brought us so much closer together."

MOTHER MASSAGE

If you become an infant massage instructor, you train parents to be their baby's massage therapist, and, occasionally, you may perform the massage yourself. With mother massage, you'll be the massage therapist. You can also be a teacher, instructing the new or expectant mom how to massage herself and the new dad to become closer with mom through healing massage.

When a woman is expecting, her body undergoes many stress-producing changes. Massage can minimize or eliminate many of the adverse effects of stress and accompanying discomforts.

Benefits of Massage to Mother

Mother massage can:

- Help prepare mother for an easier delivery
- Help to stabilize hormonal levels, making side effects of shifts in hormonal levels less severe
- Control varicose veins in the legs and reduce swelling of the legs
- Improve general circulation, thus improving circulation to the placenta
- Improve lymphatic circulation, resulting in more energy and less fatigue
- Decrease muscle strain on the lower back, abdomen, and shoulders
- Improve muscle tone
- Relax the muscles and relieve frazzled nerves

Carol Osborne-Sheets, president of Somatic Learning Associates, which provides training in mother massage, also points out the benefits of massage during labor and the postpartum period:

- During labor, massage can actually facilitate birth by helping to relieve pain and cramping and to increase relaxation. Perineal massage, which the massage therapist can teach the mother, increases relaxation of the pelvic floor and improves chances of intact perineal delivery, lessening the chances of an episiotomy.

- In the postpartum period, massage can help to restore muscle tone to its prepregnancy state. Often, new mothers continue to have a "pregnancy posture" because of weak muscles. Massage therapy can help to move her out of this by restoring balance.

The earlier during pregnancy the mother starts massage, the more comfortable her pregnancy will be, notes Carol. Usually, however, the mother will come for massage after she starts to experience discomforts. Better to get her before these discomforts start and, if possible, prevent them.

Mother Massage Techniques

Massage techniques commonly used in mother massage include Swedish strokes, Shiatsu acupressure, and reflexology.

The Swedish strokes included are effleurage, petrissage, friction, tapotement, and the nerve stroke. Effleurage is the stroke that begins and ends each treatment. It is a long, gliding movement that introduces the massage and prepares the muscles for deeper work. This may be followed by petrissage, popularly referred to as kneading. Friction is generally used in therapeutic treatments to relieve muscle spasms and tension. Tapotement, also called percussion, is performed as if playing a drum with hands or fingertips. It is a stimulatory stroke. The nerve stroke is a light, gentle fingertip glide down any part of the body. It signals the end of the massage sequence.

Using acupressure, the massage therapist presses into a specific point along the "energy meridian" to break up "energy blocks," reduce muscular adhesions, increase circulation to a particular area, and produce a relaxed sense of well-being.

Reflexology is performed as described for infant massage and involves pressing on the bottom of the feet, ostensibly to relieve toxins from the body.

What's the First Step?

Pregnancy massage therapists are, first of all, massage therapists. Massage therapists can go through a wide variety of programs; all programs need to provide a good understanding of the theory and rationale of massage, as well as education in physiology and anatomy. All massage training programs require at least 500 hours of classroom time; some require as many as 1,000 hours. Anyone interested in becoming a massage therapist—mother massage or any other kind of adult massage—should contact the American Massage Therapy Association (see Resources at the end of the chapter). This organization will provide a list of accredited programs around the country and will describe various types of massage training.

Training and Certification

Training and certification requirements vary from state to state. Some states require no training or licensing; but at least thirty states require completion of an approved training program and a certain number of hours in the classroom.

Once you've become a massage therapist, then consider moving on to mother massage. Somatic Learning Associates in La Jolla, California, has one of the largest training programs for mother massage. This program, called Bodywork for the Childbearing Year, provides training in the various techniques described earlier and targets the program specifically to mother massage. One graduate of this program, Carroll Patterson, is president of the National Association of Pregnancy Massage Therapists (see Resources at the end of the chapter). This organization can direct you to local training programs for mother massage.

Where Do I Work?

Will you be working from home? Will you go to your client's home, to a health club or local YMCA or YWCA, to a nearby hospital? That depends on your terms of employment—whether you're self-employed, working for the health club or Y, on contract with the hospital, and so on. Whatever the situation, you will require a warm, draft-free room, a mat, and, ideally, a massage surface that does not require that you bend over. You should be able to perform the massage free of distractions; next to the playroom, where baby-sitter and children are playing hide and seek, is not a good idea.

How Much Do I Charge?

The going rate for mother massage is about $50 per hour-long session. Many therapists offer discounts of perhaps 30 percent to clients willing to make a long-term commitment—say, five sessions. The goal is to get the woman in at least monthly, and perhaps weekly if she is suffering from many discomforts that can be alleviated by massage.

What Supplies Will I Need?

Supplies are basically the same for both adult and infant massage: a warm, draft-free room, a blanket, a pillow if desired, and the oils of your (and your client's) choice. Oils such as almond, peanut, safflower, and avocado are all soothing. If you or your client is interested in aromatherapy massage, more exotic oils are available. To be enjoyable, aromatherapy need only involve using scents of your choice; to be therapeutic, you may want to learn more about aromatherapy massage as a separate type of massage therapy.

Where Do I Find Clients?

Most mother massage therapists agree that the best sources of clients are midwives, obstetricians, and, occasionally, chiropractors. Because mother massage therapists try to reach clients early in the pregnancy, childbirth education classes may not be the best source. However, childbirth educators may be a valuable referral source because of contacts within health care providers and facilities.

And, not surprisingly, a major source of clients for the mother massage therapist will be satisfied clients, both from word-of-mouth recommendations and from written letters of recommendation.

The ancient art of massage provides a career opportunity that permits flexibility in hours and time. It demands a commitment to training and to promoting health and healing. Training will take time. It's not for just anybody—you must feel comfortable with this highly personal type of touch. But the rewards for the mother and the infant—and the gratification you will feel as a result—may make it worth it.

RESOURCES: INFANT MASSAGE

BOOKS

All of the following books should be available at a well-stocked bookstore. Look in the parenting section. Many of them are also available through the Gentle Touch Warehouse, listed below.

Baby Massage. Parent-Child Bonding through Touch by A.D. Auckett. New York: Newmarket Press, 1989.

Infant Massage. A Handbook for Loving Parents by Vimala Schneider McClure. New York: Bantam Books, 1989.

The Baby Book: Everything You Need to Know about Your Baby—From Birth to Age Two by William Sears and Martha Sears. Boston: Little, Brown, 1993.

Touching. The Human Significance of the Skin (3rd ed.) by Ashley Montagu. New York: Harper & Row, 1986.

ORGANIZATION

International Association of Infant Massage (IAIM)
1720 Wind Creek Circle
Suite 516
Eugene, OR 97402
888-448-9489 or 800-248-5432
The IAIM can suggest a massage instructor in your area, can provide information about how to become an infant massage instructor, and can send a list of scheduled training sessions around the country.

SUPPLIES

The Gentle Touch Warehouse
1720 Wind Creek Circle
Suite 516
Eugene, OR 97402
888-448-9489 or 800-248-5432
Supplies books, videotapes, audiotapes, and massage supplies, including essential oils. It also suggests gifts for parents.

RESOURCES: MOTHER MASSAGE

BOOKS

The Complete Book of Massage by Clare Maxwell-Hudson. London: Dorling Kindersley, 1989.

Mother Massage: A Handbook for Relieving the Discomforts of Pregnancy by Elaine Stillerman, LMT. New York: Dell, 1992.

ASSOCIATIONS

American Massage Therapy Association
820 Davis Street
Suite 100
Evanston, IL 60201-4444
773-761-2682
Provides information about becoming a licensed massage therapist—the first step to becoming a pregnancy/mother massage therapist. Can provide information about classes in your area and licensing requirements state by state.

Somatic Learning Associates
8950 Villa La Jolla Drive
Suite 2162
La Jolla, CA 92037
619-748-8827
Has certified more than 1,200 pregnancy massage therapists around the country. This program is changing as of 1997 and may split into two organizations. Therefore, details of the program not currently available. Ask for additional information when you call.

National Association of Pregnancy Massage Therapists
c/o Carroll Patterson, President
P.O. Box 9802-547
Austin, TX 78766-0802
512-323-5925

10

MAKING HOME A SAFE HAVEN: CHILDPROOFING SPECIALIST

What will you do?	Childproof homes and train parents to be safety-conscious
How many hours a week?	3–40 hours
Your work hours?	Variable; not necessarily traditional hours
Will you need licensing/certification?	None required
What can you earn?	$75–$2,500 per week
Liability insurance needed?	Required

The ultimate freelance job! You set the hours and prices and take on as much or as little work as you choose. These are some of the most attractive aspects of a childproofing business.

Childproofing is a new field. It just wasn't needed a few generations ago. Now, with tons of electrical gadgets in every household and with children being left with caregivers who may not be familiar with the home, home may not be the safe haven it should be for an infant.

As soon as baby starts crawling, the world becomes dangerous. Electrical plugs and outlets, stairs, VCRs and CD players with holes just big enough to accommodate little fingers (or Cheerios, or peanut butter sandwiches), stoves, and even pets become fascinating to the infant. Of course, there's no substitute for adult supervision to prevent accidents from happening, but even the most vigilant caretaker can become distracted for a moment. That's all it takes for potential disaster. And that's why childproofing is so crucial.

Many products are on the market to help make the home safe for baby. But finding them, installing them, and using them properly may be as tricky for a parent as opening a childproof aspirin bottle during a pounding headache.

WHY A CHILDPROOFER?

Childproofers know how an infant looks at the world. They will go into the home and crawl around on their hands and knees and will search in every corner to discover hidden dangers. But a childproofer does more than just look at the potential dangers; she knows how to avert the potential disasters there. A professional childproofer knows which safety devices are on the market, which are the best quality, where to find them, and how to install them.

Sound like a fun job? It can be. But a childproofing business requires self-education, training, marketing, and more.

If you have children, you probably did some kind of childproofing

The Beginning of a Childproofing Business

Thomas Golden and Susan Golden, both emergency department nurses, were alarmed at the large numbers of child accident victims that they were seeing in the ER (emergency room). Most of the injuries they saw were preventable. So when Susan became pregnant, the couple set out to make sure their own child didn't end up in the ER; they wanted to babyproof their home. But they found that a thorough babyproofing isn't as easy as meets the eye. Many products they felt they needed were not locally available. In other cases, such as cabinet locks, the selection of products was so enormous (there are nearly four dozen on the market), that they found selecting the appropriate one a daunting task.

If they were confused, they reasoned, many other parents must be as well. Tom Golden started Dr. Baby Proofer, Inc., a full-service babyproofing company that conducts safety assessments, teaches parents how to prevent accidents, and provides and installs safety devices. His ten-year-old business grosses six figures and has a staff of six. He now offers a training program to help others open similar businesses.

Golden did not start out with such ambitions. His original goal was to simply sell the babyproofing products that he believed were tried and true—the best cabinet latches, the safest and most reliable electrical outlet covers, and so on. But having provided this service, he found that most parents needed and were willing to pay for installation and advice as well.

Golden has fun with his business. He'll arrive at a home in a brightly colored surgeon's outfit. This puts the clients at ease. But then they get down to serious business.

Golden says that 60 percent of those requesting a safety evaluation and consultation request a full installation (that is, at least 80 percent of what is recommended); 20 percent request a partial installation and plan on doing the rest themselves; 10 percent plan on doing the entire safety installation themselves; and 10 percent do nothing with the information he has provided.

in your own home. While almost every parent is familiar with safety devices such as electrical outlet covers and safety latches for cupboards, they may not be looking beyond the obvious. For example, what about the backyard deck? A small child can slip through a railing in a moment. Safety netting may be in order. Or the stairway banister? A safety gate at the bottom may not stop a child from crawling outside the banister. Short of closing off a fireplace, is there a way to keep a fireplace hearth safe?

You can be the resource to respond to these dilemmas for new parents. You can help them make their home—and Grandma and Grandpa's home, and the babysitter's home, or the day-care center—as safe as it needs to be.

A childproofer may offer three main services:

- The safety assessment—determining what needs to be done
- The consultation and safety demonstration—discussing with the parents what they need to make their home safer and demonstrating and/or providing safety products for the parents to purchase
- Installation of the recommended devices—completing the part of the job that the parents may feel they can take on themselves, little realizing that this can be the trickiest aspect of a thorough childproofing.

Each of these services can generate a separate fee, and one can be done without the other two. But a package deal including the assessment, consultation and demonstration, and installation should be the goal.

The Safety Assessment

This involves inspecting the home, checklist in hand, and thoroughly assessing dangers that may lurk there. In this portion of the service, you will be getting on hands and knees, so dress comfortably.

Among the safety aspects to consider:

- Is the house equipped with an intercom to monitor the child?
- Are electrical outlets covered?
- Are appliances completely out of reach or secured to a surface, and are cords inaccessible?
- Do all windows have gates or guards, and can the windows, gates, and guards be securely locked?
- Are clear glass doors on cabinets marked with opaque tape to prevent baby from crashing into them?
- Do cabinet doors have childproof latches?
- Are stairwells blocked off with a gate? Are banisters protected with netting so baby can't slip through?
- Is the hot water heater set at 120°F? (In most unbabyproofed houses, it is conventionally set at 140°F or even higher.)
- Are sharp table corners protected by padding?
- Are plastic bags of any type—dry cleaning, food, and so on—out of reach?
- Are all small objects and foods such as popcorn and nuts out of the child's reach? Do playthings or upholstery contain buttons?
- Is pet food set out for the family pet in a place not available to baby?
- Are sharp objects—knives, scissors and so on—stored and kept out of reach of baby?
- Does the toilet seat have a safety latch?
- Are all medicines out of reach and locked away?

- Is baby's crib free of pillows and toys that baby could roll on or under? Are the crib bars narrowly spaced so baby can't slip through?
- Are emergency numbers listed at each phone?
- Does the medicine cabinet contain a bottle of ipecac syrup?

This is not a comprehensive list, but it should give you a good idea of the pitfalls that can await a toddler.

A thorough safety assessment might take half a day, depending, of course, on the size and age of the home (older homes may present a particular challenge) and the dangers that may lurk there. In each room, in each hallway, on each staircase, *document* all of your findings on the safety checklist.

Next Step: The Consultation

When you've finished the safety assessment, you'll sit down with the parent or caregiver to review your findings. Start out by providing, for each phone, stickers containing emergency numbers and spaces for their pediatrician's number and the poison control number. Give them publications from the U.S. Consumer Products Safety Commission (see Resources at the end of the chapter). These steps will help them to understand your commitment to their child's safety.

Then, review the checklist thoroughly, pointing out safety flaws that can be rectified without installation (for example, removing pillows and stuffed animals from baby's crib) and then moving on to recommendations of safety device installations. Bring samples of the most common devices you recommend for installation—cupboard latches, doorknob covers, outlet covers, spout guards, and so on. Don't come weighted down with dozens of items; bring only samples. After all, you don't necessarily want the parents to buy on the spot; you want them to order the devices from you and then to have you install them. But provide them with a price list of items you do have available, and make sure that you'll be able to order them promptly. More later about where to order safety devices to sell and supply to your clients.

This consultation session may be the end of your services to the family. Indeed, this may be the extent of your business. But strive for more; safety installations can be the most lucrative part of a babyproofing business. Try to persuade your customers to purchase some of the safety devices you've recommended—preferably from you, of course. You will need to stress the importance of reliable installation. Do-it-yourselfers may balk; but parents working outside the home and those who may not be so handy may be glad to have a pro come in and install the devices just as they were meant to be installed.

Remind clients, too, of dangers that may lurk at the grandparents' house. If baby is a frequent visitor, they may want a safety assessment there. Is baby in a day-care facility during the day? If your customers are happy with your assessment of their house, they may recommend you to their caregiver's facility.

The Installation

If you make the safety installation part of your services, you'll have to know how to install all of the devices you're recommending. You must be not just familiar with but adept at installing a wide variety of devices. You'll be going to the home, cordless drill and screwdriver in hand, to install the devices. No room for klutzes here. Don't worry—you don't need to be a seasoned carpenter or an engineer. Most devices are meant to be installed by parents just like those who are your customers; but it's your responsibility to provide the highest quality installation expected of a babyproofing professional. Before you begin, alert customers when you'll have to drill or hammer into walls, floors, and furniture. Don't surprise them.

One important caution: Sorry to say, in this litigious society, some parents may hold you liable if materials malfunction or if baby is able to outwit the safety devices. While this is unlikely, protect yourself with a contract limiting liability; you will need to consult a lawyer to check on the wording, but the contract should contain a clause noting your limits of liability and noting the parents' responsibility to make sure all items are in working order. For example:

> Your baby's safety is a major concern for all parents and caretakers. The installer recommends that you (Owner) periodically inspect all products and devices installed for proper function and possible signs of wear and tear.
>
> Owner acknowledges that children differ greatly from one another, and, therefore, it is impossible for Installer to predict all potential safety hazards in the home. Owner agrees that any product, service, or recommendation made or provided by Installer cannot guarantee against accidental death or injury that may occur in the home with relation to any product, service, or recommendation made or provided by Installer.

This wording and the limits of liability will vary from state to state for a childproofing business, and no such business can be 100 percent protected; but this contract will state in writing that parents must be responsible for maintaining the safety of their home.

You will certainly want to carry liability insurance if you're doing installation. (Nurses have a big advantage here, because liability insurance for self-employed nurses generally costs about one-tenth of that for other self-employed persons.) On the other hand, it's not such a good idea to volunteer the information that you're insured; again, sorry to say, litigious societies tend to act on those who are protected in this manner.

You should also consider incorporating your business. That way, in the unlikely event that you are sued, you are less likely to lose personal assets.

WHAT'S THE FIRST STEP?

It's likely from your own experience with trying to babyproof your own home that you know there's much to learn. No certification or licensing is required to start a babyproofing business, but you'll be considered more of a professional—and lessen liability problems—if you've been through a recognized program of baby safety. A good start would be checking with the American Red Cross to locate infant safety programs.

If you're not quite ready to go into business for yourself, check the Yellow Pages and local parent magazines to see if any babyproofing businesses are already established in your area. See if they're interested in hiring you to do safety assessments, consultations, or installations. This might give you the opportunity to see if you like the field. Whether you then decide to establish your own business depends on how much you've decided you like the work and whether there's a big enough market for another babyproofing business. Chances are, however, that you won't find a babyproofing service by name; only a few hundred businesses are known to be devoted specifically to this specialty, although carpenters or nurses or paramedics may have less ambitious services that may be hidden under a different business title.

TRAINING AND CERTIFICATION

Currently, there is only one training program specifically designed for persons interested in starting a babyproofing business. But childproofing is a new field. More programs may develop. (In fact, one training program we contacted has already folded.) Thomas Golden, R.N., president and owner of the extremely successful Dr. Baby Proofer in Dallas (see Resources at the end of the chapter), has developed a five-day program, which he conducts in Dallas. He is the sole instructor. He describes the first day of the program as a didactic, where he enumerates the pleasures and pitfalls of running a small business of this nature. The second and third days are down-to-work days—students go to two homes and perform complete safety installations. One of the homes is a new home and one is older. Golden wants to show that every home has a different personality, and many older homes were subject to different safety concerns when they were built. On the fourth day, students perform two safety assessments in two homes. The fifth day is a debriefing day where resources are discussed and safety information is reviewed.

This program wins rave reviews from former students. Be aware, however, that it is very expensive. Your week in Dallas will cost about $7,500. Further, because licensing or certification is not required, completion of a course is not necessary to start your business. But it is one way to jump start it.

Golden is also president of a baby-safety organization—the newly founded International Association for Child Safety (IACS) (see Resources at the end of the chapter). This fledgling organization's stated purpose is to promote networking among the members of the small but growing field of babyproofing. Started just a few years ago, the IACS plans to have annual or biannual meetings in conjunction with the Juvenile Products Manufacturers Association meeting. Eventually, it plans to endorse quality baby safety products. For now, it produces a monthly newsletter to link the members (currently about forty) to each other and to apprise the membership of new developments. This organization may be a good resource for deciding which safety devices are the best, for learning where they can be found, and for determining what current babyproofers are doing and what they charge.

HOW MUCH DO I CHARGE?

For a three- or four-hour initial safety assessment, you may want to charge a standard flat fee of $75. The cost of a complete babyproofing audit, consultation, and installation obviously depends on the size of the home, the hazards uncovered, and the extent of your services requested. Installation can take anywhere from three hours to two days. An hourly fee of about $30 for installation may mean a total fee from about $100 to $500. Purchases of supplies may run anywhere from under $100 to several hundred. Golden says that a childproofing can run to $1,200 with his full range of services, and he has charged as much as $5,000.

What you should charge for the safety devices you supply depends on your own cost, plus a markup. You'll want to be competitive, of course; see what similar devices cost in local stores. Find a wholesale supplier who can sell for less so that you can make a modest profit on the items you supply.

You'll want to keep enough supplies on hand to service your clients; nothing's more frustrating for your client than deciding to buy something and then finding out it's not available. You do not need to keep a large inventory, but you will need reliable suppliers who can ship your supplies via one- or two-day service.

The tricky part is deciding which devices and brands to recommend. Dozens of cupboard safety latches are available. How to choose? Remember the U.S. Consumer Products Safety Commission is an excellent resource for determining if any devices have been found faulty. Watch out via the Consumer Products Safety Commission for recalls or withdrawals of any baby safety devices. Regularly read *Consumer Reports*—this monthly magazine, published by Consumers Union (see Resources at the end of the chapter), provides information on independent testing of a variety of devices as well as on recalls.

WHAT SUPPLIES WILL I NEED?

Less than you might think: letterhead, business cards, a phone, and one of each product that you'll likely be selling. No need to get bogged down with inventory; keep the cash flow positive, especially when you're starting out.

Supplies You'll Need for Your Clients

Safety latches for drawers and cabinets
Refrigerator latches
Safety plugs for electrical outlets
Edge cushions for table corners and fireplace hearths
Doorknob covers
Cushioned spout guards for bathtubs
Stove knob covers
Corner guards
Safety gates
Safety netting
Lid lock for toilet seats
Nonskid rubber bath mat
TV/VCR covers and locks
Hearth guard
Netting for decks and stairways
Screen guards
Rubber stripping for stairs

And be prepared to recommend:

Car seats
Cordless phones
Nonskid rug pads
Intercom or baby monitor
Fire extinguishers
Smoke detectors
Carbon monoxide detectors

If installation is going to be part of your services, you'll need to have tools for installation and know how to use them. Invest in some good cordless tools (a drill and a screwdriver), a hammer or two, a metal tape measure, some regular screwdrivers, and perhaps a level.

HOW DO I FIND CLIENTS?

Not surprisingly, a major source of clients is word of mouth. Consider each client a source for other clients. Be certain to follow up on all installations—perhaps at intervals of one, two, and three months. If a device has been damaged, replace it at no cost. Clients are often so delighted with your concern that they will tell their friends. Be sure to have clients who are satisfied with your services write letters of recommendation. Show these to potential clients at the initial consultation and to potential networking resources.

Pediatricians' offices can be an extremely effective source of clients. Send local pediatricians safety information for their patients; most physicians tend to be disease-oriented but may not have had much training in accident prevention. Passing on information about safety and about your services is a beneficial add-on to their practice. After sending them materials, contact them and offer tips and information, which they can pass along to their patients. Regularly supply the doctors with informational brochures, leaving a space with your name and information about your services.

Also, contact childbirth educators and parent educators in your area. Again, share safety information with them and send them a supply of cards. Offer safety checklists, but allow space to promote your own services. Offer to speak at their classes. Stress the advantages of professional installation of baby safety devices.

Also, make yourself known to community and parent groups and offer to speak on safety. You may want to do this in conjunction with a video or with demonstrations of safety devices. Again, stress the advantages of an independent eye coming in to assess the safety of the home and to install the safety devices; it's easy for parents to overlook the obvious. Run ads in local parenting magazines and community newspapers. You can generate some great publicity by "goodwill" installations—doing an installation in a church nursery or a foster care home free of charge.

Do you want to give it a shot? This is a great job for a nurse who is a mother now staying at home, a carpenter, or any enterprising person with an interest in and commitment to baby safety. Start by assessing the safety of your own home. Practice on a friend's or a relative's home. See how you like it. Go from there.

RESOURCES

VIDEOTAPE

Safe at Home ($19.95)
Pacific Film Group
P.O. Box 1082
Pacific Palisades, CA 90272
800-905-9997

ORGANIZATIONS

International Association for Child Safety
P.O. Box 595834
Dallas, TX 75359-5831
888-677-IACS
Dues: $25
The only organization for professional babyproofers.

National Safe Kids Campaign
111 Michigan Avenue, NW
Washington, DC 20010

U.S. Consumer Products Safety Commission (CPSC)
Document #206: Baby Safety Checklist
Document #5082: Baby Product Safety Tips—Safety Alert
CPSC Hotline: 800-638-2772
The U.S. Consumer Products Safety Commission protects the public from the unreasonable risk of injury or death from 15,000 types of consumer products under the agency's jurisdiction.

The Injury Prevention Program (TIPP)
American Academy of Pediatrics
800-433-9016
The American Academy of Pediatrics provides baby safety advice and information. Call the 800 number listed to find out what's available.

SUPPLIES

Perfectly Safe Catalog
7835 Freedom Avenue NW
North Canton, OH 44720
800-837-KIDS

Right Start Catalog
800-548-8531

Childproofer
Online Catalog and Child Safety Education Corner
World Wide Web site: http://www.childproofer.com
800-374-2525
P.O. Box 14718
Santa Rosa, CA 95402
This company has a novel standard for testing all products available: "Sam's Safety Scale," which was developed by having a child test the product. The scale rates items from * (very easy for a child to master) to **** (very difficult for a child to master). You can order a free catalog from the 800 number or through the Web site.

Safe 'N Sound Kids Corp.
World Wide Web site: http://www.safensoundkids.com
e-mail: safetytots@aol.com
888-252-BABY or 718-252-BABY

INDEX

ABOUT THE AUTHORS

Suzanne B. Robotti founded *Childbirth Instructor Magazine* in 1990 and has been the publisher ever since. In 1994, she helped launch *Baby Magazine*, and in 1996 she took over the *Bounty Infant Care Guide* and oversaw its redesign into *Baby Magazine's Infant Care Guide*. Robotti is currently principal and group publisher of the Baby Publishing Group, which comprises all three magazines. She lives in Manhattan with her husband.

Margaret Ann Inman has been a health and medical writer for more than twenty years. She is the founding editor of *Childbirth Instructor Magazine*; she was also editor of *Directions*, a newsletter for administrators of childbirth education programs. Currently a freelance journalist, Inman is a reporter and writer for professional publications such as *Cardiovascular Horizons* and *Pulmonary Reviews*. She has written both public and professional educational materials for the American Heart Association and was managing editor of its flagship journal, *Circulation*. She lives in Brooklyn with her husband, a jazz musician.